FIELD NOTES FROM AN UNINTENTIONAL BIRDER

FIELD NOTES FROM AN

a memoir

UNINTENTIONAL BIRDER

JULIA ZARANKIN

Douglas & McIntyre

Douglas and McIntyre (2013) Ltd.
P.O. Box 219, Madeira Park, BC, VON 2HO
www.douglas-mcintyre.com

Edited by Caroline Skelton
Cover design by Setareh Ashrafologhalai
Text design by Brianna Cerkiewicz
Printed and bound in Canada
Printed on acid-free paper certified by the Forest Stewardship Council

Douglas and McIntyre acknowledges the support of the Canada Council for the Arts, the Government of Canada and the Province of British Columbia through the BC Arts Council.

Library and Archives Canada Cataloguing in Publication

Title: Field notes from an unintentional birder : a memoir / by Julia Zarankin.

Names: Zarankin, Julia, 1974- author.

Description: Includes bibliographical references.

Identifiers: Canadiana (print) 20200192221 | Canadiana (ebook) 2020019223X | ISBN 9781771622486 (softcover) | ISBN 9781771622493 (HTML)

Subjects: LCSH: Zarankin, Julia, 1974- | LCSH: Bird watchers—Biography. | LCSH: Bird watching. | LCGFT: Autobiographies.

Classification: LCC QL677.5 .Z37 2020 | DDC 598.072/34—dc23

To Leon, for becoming an almost-birder,
and
in memory of Bronwyn Dalziel (1991–2016)

Contents

Interior Decorating

WHEN I WAS GROWING UP, DECEMBER WAS THE MONTH OF the year when my parents received classical music kitsch as gifts. So many items appeared in our house, given in earnest by their piano students, that we didn't know what to do with them all. Plastic busts of Schubert and Beethoven hardly qualified as easy re-gift items, and there were only so many mugs with eighth-note handles and images of the first four notes of Beethoven's Fifth Symphony that fit into our cupboards. Most of our notepads were of the "Chopin Liszt" variety, tea towels had treble clefs, and numerous miniature crystal grand pianos adorned the real pianos in our home; some clever friends of my parents' even gave them pillowcases with *Encore!* written in fiery cursive script and nestled into a musical staff. We displayed the gifts at Christmas, since they added a layer of festivity to our secular household, and then, shortly after the holidays, we sent them into hiding until the following year.

I swore that when I grew up and had a place of my own, mine would be a home without tchotchkes, and sans treble clefs and composers. For a while, life proceeded according to plan. As a graduate student and junior faculty member, I kept my apartment spartan, my walls bare. When I moved in with my husband, things began to slip. Initially, I mocked his Texas longhorn, threw away his glow-in-the-dark sparkly Eiffel Tower wall hangings and relegated the romantic candelabras with scented candles to our storage locker, but as an act of compromise I had to accept the imposing unicorn poster that hung over my computer. My husband also came with a non-negotiable collection of some three hundred stone elephants of varying sizes, a semi–life-sized plush tiger-and-leopard pair, and tiger tea towels.

And then something even stranger happened. I discovered birds. Within a year, the barometric pressure in our apartment shifted. Stuffed-animal squeaky hooded warblers learned to coexist with tigers; bird-shaped vases stood next to the elephant-shaped salt shaker; sculpted owls flirted with the faux-malachite elephant's plastic tusks.

And in my study, the unicorn gave way to something more frightening: a pile of bird-themed stationery of every persuasion and a shelf dedicated to field guides, from the general *Birds of North America* to the specific—books dedicated to sparrows, shorebirds, warblers, bird behaviour and the like. Not to mention the nondescript felt bird, handcrafted by my sister, the two paintings of birds by David Morrisseau, and the stained-glass owl made by my grandmother when she was ninety-three years old.

Some days, I walk into my own study and wonder how I ended up here, with parrot notebooks, a collection of bird-themed T-shirts, subscriptions to *Living Bird, Birding, Bird Studies Canada, Bird Watcher's Digest* and *BirdWatching*, and memberships in more conservation organizations than I can count. There was a time when I subscribed to the *Slavic and East European Journal, The Russian Review* and *Canadian Slavic Studies.* But a decade ago, the tectonic plates of my world started to shift.

"I think your decor has surpassed our treble clefs and eighth-note mugs," my father said. Little did he know that my closet held a dozen bird T-shirts, an owl skirt and a hummingbird earring-and-necklace set, and that I constantly scoured the Internet for more.

I had also begun amassing catalogues of scopes and binoculars and learning all sorts of optic lore. I found myself discussing Carl Zeiss, one of the fathers of German high-end optics, with nothing short of sensual innuendo. I knew the contours of the face of David Sibley, God of the Modern Field Guide, as if he were one of my close relatives. In fact, I *saw* David Sibley's face much more often than I saw my own cousins because I perused his book most evenings before bed. Peering into his eyes, I found myself wishing that he would ditch that navy turtleneck he wears in many of his photos, and perhaps don new glasses that were a bit more in vogue.

Who had I become exactly?

A Semi-Retired Hen

IN 2013, WHILE VISITING FRIENDS ON DENMAN ISLAND, IN British Columbia, I nearly bought a half-dozen semi-retired hens. I didn't wake up one morning craving chickens, but when I read the classifieds-cum-for-sale last page of the island newsletter and saw the ad for hens, the six sad, soon to be abandoned, partially useless birds beckoned to me. It wasn't that I had any need for chickens or that I had properly entertained the logistics of transporting a flock from Denman Island back to Toronto, or that I could find a place for them in my eighth-floor condo, or that I even understood the meaning of "semi-retired hens." But something in the wording, in their very existence, struck me as essential.

Five years prior, I wouldn't have paid the chickens any heed. Their existence would have passed me by entirely. And yet now, the idea of hens in mid-life concerned me directly. Their reproductive years likely behind them, how would these six hens now behave? Would they sit around, book-club style, discussing the finer points of literature? Or would they contemplate the aging process and possibly talk about recalibrating their lives, perhaps entertain a new hobby, attempt to make sense of life now that they found themselves past their legitimate, biological prime? Or might one of them unexpectedly get a second wind, move on to wider horizons and, contrary to natural tendencies, continue to lay eggs?

I didn't buy them, but for half a day, all I could talk about were the hens. In the end, I bought a bantam chicken in the form of a four-by-four-inch oil painting. Not for its technical mastery, but for this peculiar animal in profile, my new talisman, looking straight ahead, venturing forth with confidence into a new chapter of her life. She now lives in my study, on my desk, next to a hawk print, a felt chickadee and not one but two bird calendars, and under an enormous Sibley's "Backyard Birds" poster for eastern North America. I sometimes wonder if she is happy here, in this strange menagerie of avifauna.

I COULDN'T HELP BUT SEE A SHADE OF MYSELF IN THESE CHICK-ens. Instinctively, I wanted to be privy to their lives, to eavesdrop on their conversations and behavioural patterns to better understand my own predicament. In my mid-thirties, I had published an essay called "The Neutral Decade," where I summed things up with the phrase "nothing hurts and nothing feels great." In the decade since writing that, I had come to terms with the fact that I would not become a mother, and that a career I had worked toward for over a decade was not an ideal match. Now I had reached my forties and a peculiar awareness of mid-life lurked everywhere; mortality appeared on my radar full-force. On the day of my nephew's birth, it dawned on me that when he was my age, I would be eighty-two years old, and with that I had the hauntingly banal realization that he would never know me as I knew myself right now: mostly young, mostly healthy, mostly content, but a little bit at sea and a little bit troubled by the reality of time passing and the knowledge that things might never be this good again. I had months of crippling fear when I would stare at my husband, knowing that we were fortunate for so many reasons, including the wild unicorn of having found one another, and in spite of that fortune, I still worried: *Is this it? Is this what it means to live?*

Everywhere I looked, I saw chickens. As I reread Chekhov's *Uncle Vanya* for an adult education class I was teaching, I noticed that as the world crumbles around the characters and they are left with nothing, their servant, Marina, keeps on, *literally*, feeding the chickens. What were chickens doing in Chekhov? I had always focused on the play's larger message and hadn't ever paid much attention to the chickens. Yet there they were. And rereading the play, I saw that the chickens—maybe Marina's were also semi-retired?—depicted continuity, the small, mundane actions that we cannot live without, the ones that give contour to our lives.

I wondered: What does a semi-retired—biologically speaking—woman in mid-life do? How does she fill the void she didn't even know she had?

I DISCOVERED BIRDS WHEN MANY THINGS IN MY LIFE SEEMED disappointing: I had emerged from both a career that I'd worked extremely hard for, only to realize that it didn't make me happy, and a marriage that had fallen apart; I had just entered into a new relationship that I wasn't sure I had the force to sustain and second-guessed myself at every turn; and the reality that I would never have kids had finally set in.

At a career crossroads, I ended up back in Toronto, my hometown, which isn't truly my hometown because I come from a country that is no longer. To call Kharkiv my hometown would be absurd, since I last saw the city in 1978, at the age of almost four, back when it was called Kharkov, when Ukraine was a republic of the Soviet Union, when I wore saggy, scratchy woollen tights and talked to imaginary friends on the telephone for hours. And to call Kharkov my hometown would have been doubly absurd because as a small child, I shuttled back and forth between Odessa, where my maternal grandparents lived; Leningrad, where my mother studied; Petrozavodsk, where my father worked; and back to Kharkov, where my paternal grandmother lived; I was already a migratory species before I knew such a thing existed. Later, I acquired other hometowns: Vienna, for a short period that I barely remember beyond our immigrant compound and trips to the market to sell our precious obsolete Soviet electronics and tool sets; Edmonton, where I learned English; Vancouver, where I might have discovered the outdoors, but instead acquired French; and finally Toronto, where we settled in 1987. I left the city for university in the United States, swore I'd never return to this provincial backwater, stayed away for graduate school at Princeton and a post-doc at Stanford, and then accepted a job in mid-Missouri, the job I had once dreamt of. When things no longer held together, I left my job and returned to the closest thing I had to a hometown.

At loose ends, I started auditioning hobbies, from bookmaking to letterpress to cycling, hiking and pottery—waiting for something to stick. I thought back to an old housemate I'd had in graduate school, who used to set up a spotting scope and watch ducks on Lake Carnegie from our balcony, jotting down observations, counting species. Not once did I think to look through his scope, but I spent hours sitting on the sofa reading and watching him watch birds on weekend mornings.

And then I thought back to another moment, at a youth hostel in Point Reyes, California, when my sister and I accidentally ended up in one of the birding meccas of the western United States. I'd been drawn to Point Reyes for the rugged seashore, dunes and remote lighthouse. My sister came along for the ride. We ended up exploring none of those things because of high winds that blocked the road to the lighthouse, and the mild boredom that ensued. As it grew dark, we inadvertently tumbled into a conversation with a couple from the United Kingdom, clad in multipocketed khaki vests, pants tucked into socks, who had travelled the world in search of birds. They'd been to India, South America and parts of the South Pacific, they'd been all over Africa, and now they'd come to Point Reyes in search of New World species. I wanted to hear about the Taj Mahal, about safari adventures, but they ignored my questions and told me about exquisite birds and rare plumages and remarkable additions to their life lists. My sister yawned uncontrollably, my eyes glazed over, and they kept talking at a frenetic clip, one interrupting the other to correct a misstep in genus, a wrong subspecies, while I tried, unsuccessfully, to bring the conversation back to zebras or, at the very least, Indian food—two things I could at least visualize.

As we attempted to abort the conversation, the hardy woman stepped out onto the porch and waved us over, "If you're very, very quiet, you just might see a bird."

A bird was calling, or hooting, or making some noise I didn't yet have a word for.

We shushed and stood there for a few minutes, behind the enthusiastic birdwatcher, before sneaking off to bed. She stayed on for over an hour, until she caught movement in the reeds beyond the hostel, satisfied with a glimpse of a nocturnal species. For the rest of our trip, my sister and I repeated the woman's line to one another, without knowing what it meant, and without wanting to know.

A FEW MONTHS AFTER MOVING BACK TO TORONTO, I ADMITted to my sister that my attempts to fill my hobby void hadn't amounted to much.

"What are you looking for?"

"Something that will exercise my patience."

"That's it?"

"And bring me peace, without having to do yoga."

She looked at me and, before laughing, whispered, in a monotone faux-British accent, "If you're very, very quiet, you just might see a bird."

Spark Bird

PART OF ME BELIEVES I WAS DESTINED TO DISCOVER BIRDS, that it would have happened one way or another. I mean, what non-birder would start sporting a Tilley hat with pride at sixteen? My sister, who is eight years younger, also reminds me that I've been keeping lists—of trips taken, movies seen, books read, plays watched, great meals consumed—for as long as she can remember, and that I started wearing sensible shoes years before I actually needed to, orthopaedically speaking: they just felt right.

It began with a few innocuous Internet searches. First, I made the mistake of searching "Birdwatching Toronto" and was overwhelmed: dozens of options, from the professional to the amateur, including something called the Toronto Ornithological Club, which required people to have a "birding resumé" to be considered for active membership. This might be too much for me, I thought. I let a few months pass, and then tried again.

"Birdwatching class Toronto" yielded slightly more specificity, but the classes had either already passed or they sounded too complex, and I was hardly ready for a multi-week commitment; they offered outings to places I'd never heard of, lists of birds with names that read like poetry in a foreign language: *red-breasted merganser, Carolina wren, Bohemian waxwing*. I tried the terms "inexperienced beginner birdwatcher hobby," but the search presented me with cognitive research and scholarly articles; "stressed desperate mid-life crisis birdwatching class beginner Toronto" took me in a whole other direction and revealed a completely different kind of spectator sport. I quickly removed "stressed desperate mid-life crisis" and ended up with a more palatable list of options. I finally chose the group with the simplest description and the most colourful pictures, run by someone named Brete. Within a few weeks, I had committed to an outing and set my alarm clock for 6:00 a.m., the earliest I'd been awake since marching-band days in university.

The night before I was to meet the group at dawn in a deserted parking lot, my husband asked, "Do you even know where you're going?"

"A parking lot at Martin Grove Collegiate Institute, and from there I'll follow them. They said something about Kipling and Lake Ontario and something about grebes," I said. "No, I have no idea where I'm actually going."

"How long are you going out for?"

"I'll probably be back by nine. How long can people stare at birds?" That my husband didn't question my hobby search—that he didn't even ask if I was sure that this new birding thing was what I wanted, that he simply went along with it and accepted that he would wake up earlier on a Saturday than on a weekday, and that although I said "back by nine" and I'd likely be back by noon—were among the reasons why our relationship had survived the three-month mark, then the six-month mark, then the year-long mark, and by the time I set my alarm clock I realized that I had stopped counting the months.

I HAD NO TROUBLE RECOGNIZING THE GROUP IN THE PARKing lot. Cargo pants tucked into socks and signature off-white multipocketed vests, which I recognized from the times I'd Googled "birdwatchers," each of the half-dozen people huddled around their cars wore at least one item of bird-themed clothing, ranging from a subtle baseball cap with a woodpecker on it to a more boisterous sweatshirt featuring a giant red bird with black wings, so bright I wondered for a minute if the bird could be real. I looked around for the leader while I tried to make sense of their optics-talk; questions of magnification and the optical quality of Vortex versus Eagle Eye passed me by completely, but I understood enough to nod in appreciation when Lucy, a petite retired high school teacher, showed off her recently purchased high-end Swarovski binoculars. She later admitted, with a mischievous smile, that she'd bought them with money she had set aside for a sofa.

I knew the leader had arrived once a rusty Toyota pulled up, and everyone said, "There's Brete." A six-foot-tall high school math and science teacher, Brete wore sweatpants with a Norwegian knit sweater and a baseball cap with yet another bird on it; initially stern, his face lit up when he said, "I read a pretty good report this morning. Let's head to Kipling Spit."

Though the references to a report and to Kipling Spit, the name Brete still used to refer to Colonel Samuel Smith Park, were both lost on me, I introduced myself, reminded him of the e-mail I'd sent a few days earlier, and sheepishly admitted that I was a complete beginner.

"Not to worry—folks in our group have varying degrees of experience. I mean, there isn't a single person here who can ID all the warblers."

"Uh...a warbler?" I knew ducks and pigeons and owls existed, but what were warblers?

"Wow. You weren't kidding when you said beginner."

"Nope."

"Do you have binoculars?"

I shook my head.

"That might be a good place to start," said Brete with a chuckle, which I thought might be code for "Who is this interloper, how did she find me on the Internet and why on earth did I ever e-mail her back when she clearly said 'she didn't know a thing about birds?'"

Once we got into our respective cars, our cavalcade of birders thundered down the highway until we reached a park at the foot of Kipling Avenue, where the city meets Lake Ontario, and where, according to the report Brete had read on the ONTBIRDS listserv, a western grebe had recently been seen. A kind gentleman named Benito, draped in a long-lensed camera and binoculars, and with a spotting scope casually resting on his shoulder, let me borrow his spare binoculars, which he alternately called his bins or binocs or glasses.

The binoculars were heavy around the neck. The last time I had used binoculars seriously was when my family lived in Vancouver. As a child, I used to plant myself at the living-room window for hours, spying on our neighbour Mary through my parents' theatre glasses. I had memorized the layout of Mary's living room across the street and delighted in knowing the sequence of TV shows she watched: *The Brady Bunch* followed by *Wheel of Fortune*, with a break for Ovaltine in between and, after supper on Thursdays, *Jeopardy!* and *Knight Rider*.

"I want to live with Mary," I told my parents. My mother stared at me nervously.

"But just the other day, you said she was boring."

"I like how she does the same thing every night and even eats the same food." Mary was the only person I had ever surveyed this closely, and I associated the constancy of her everyday routine with the idea of having a real home.

"Enough with those binoculars," she said.

"She's going to watch *The Love Boat* at eight o'clock tonight."

"No more binoculars." And the same evening, the theatre glasses disappeared.

This time I didn't feel as confident. As we walked out to the lake, people started shouting words that I couldn't process: "Northern shoveler! Red-breasted merganser, American wigeon! Bufflehead, long-tailed duck!" The binoculars wobbled in my hands. High winds accosted me and when I tried to focus the lenses, my eyes watered; the second I glimpsed a duck, it dove and left me staring at the hyperactive early-April waves on Lake Ontario. "Wait, look," Brete shouted, "I think I got it, horned grebe, horned grebe, over there, next to the pied-billed grebe, you can't miss it, to the right of the dozens, no, hundreds of red-necked grebes out there, oh wait, oh my god, is that a western grebe? Are you seeing the grebes, Julia? It's not every day you get four species in one place."

My mind bobbed in and out of awareness amidst this sea of names. I nodded, but my binoculars were pointed at the CN Tower, the only thing I could safely identify on the horizon.

"What's a grebe?"

"Start with the red-necked grebes. There are close to five hundred of them out there," Brete replied. "Can't miss them—gorgeous rust-coloured neck, and look at that elongated bill! It's a textbook grebe, no doubt about it."

I located the mass of waterfowl, but in the dull light couldn't detect anything remotely rust-coloured, and all the bills looked identical to my untrained eye.

On our way back to the cars, my extremities frozen from standing still in gale-like winds, I wondered how many more hours of staring at dark blobs on the water I could withstand. Disenchanted, I was preparing my exit speech to the group, when we stopped near a bush and someone called out, "Red-winged blackbird."

I almost didn't look because the thought of lifting the binoculars to my eyes brought with it a slight wave of nausea. But the bird stood still, balancing on a cattail, and I managed the trifecta of raising the binoculars, focusing them and finding the desired object magnified in my field of vision.

"What *is* that?" I gasped, nearly blinded by the unexpected vermillion patches on the blackbird's epaulets. I watched as the bird threw back its head, opened wide its beak and let out a sound so primal it left me marvelling: this was as close as I'd ever stand to dinosaurs. If this bird had been here all along, I thought, what else had I been missing?

The Wrong Kind of Science

WHEN I WAS A CHILD, I GREW UP WITH BROWN-PAPER-wrapped packages sent from the Soviet Union by my grandmother. My grandparents were refuseniks—Russian Jews denied visas to leave the Soviet Union. Over the course of our nine-year separation, they sent the contents of their bookshelves, kitchen cupboards and linen closet piecemeal. Every three months or so a package would arrive, decorated with dozens of stamps featuring a man named Lenin or famous cosmonauts, pioneer heroes, hydroelectric plants, Soviet athletes.

These parcels arrived from people I knew only from photographs. I knew that I was born in a country one could no longer travel to. Even calling involved a multiday ritual. My mother would send my grandmother a telegram in the middle of the week to suggest a time for a prearranged telephone rendezvous. A telegram would follow in return, the next day. *Budu,* she would respond—I'll be there. Laconic, pronoun-less verbs in upper-case transliterated Russian showed up on our doorstep. Then, the following Sunday morning, she and my grandfather would walk the three kilometres from their apartment to the telephone post and wait for our call. Knowing how my grandmother now gets dressed up for doctor appointments and arrives an hour early (*You never know,* she says in the same dreamy tone she uses to remind me that a visit to the doctor merits my *best underwear*), I'm sure she and my grandfather must have left their apartment in their best clothes. It would have been an hour and a half of preparations for a telephone exchange that lasted no longer than ten minutes.

I found the conversations nerve-racking. My mother woke me up in the middle of the night for my performance of the rehearsed lines on tiptoes—*Thank you for all the presents! The sweater will fit me in a few years. I miss you! I love you! Kisses!*—but I would bite my nails in fear of a potential question that I'd answer with the wrong Russian case ending or an incorrect verb form. The connection sounded like static, we had to scream into the phone, and just as my grandparents shouted back, our own echoes would accost us. I envied friends at school with grandmothers who baked them cookies and braided their hair; mine gave me a stomach ache, talked incessantly about the various ailments I'd suffered from as a toddler, inquired as to whether ballet lessons had helped correct my posture and pigeon-toed gait, and wondered how it could be that at age ten I hadn't yet read all of Jack London.

Once, my mother called the operator and opened, as usual, with her stock phrase: "I'd like to place a person-to-person call to Russia."

"Prussia?" The operator asked.

"No, not Prussia, *Russia*. There is no Prussia anymore," my mother explained, as if she had historical clairvoyance and could sense that within the next ten years, the country she was calling would also cease to exist.

THE ONLY THING MORE TAXING THAN TALKING TO MY GRAND-parents was writing to them.

In my letters to them, I waged a war against my mother's red pen. *Remember the accusative ending for animate nouns! "Where" takes the prepositional case. Did you not memorize the list of verbal exceptions that require an* e *even when it's pronounced* u? *You forgot the spelling rule after sibilants!*

By the time I'd made all the requisite corrections, I'd lost track of the grandmother I was writing to in the first place. *You forgot to thank them for the books!*

Grammar books, a primer of microbes, English translations of didactic Russian poetry—as if the originals weren't bad enough. Collected works of Pushkin and Gogol for my parents. My grandmother was slowly sending the contents of her bookshelf, along with anything else she could find for me at the black market or through her connections.

"They don't look very interesting."

"Your grandmother stood in line for them for hours."

"For those boring books with awful pictures?"

"Just thank her."

We put the books on the bookshelves, happy to receive packages from a faraway country but also disappointed that the contents of the package held so little interest. The prickly Yugoslavian sweaters and wool underwear that reached my knees (to protect my *woman parts*), cotton nightgowns made in China, metres of crepe de Chine, bed sheets designed for different-sized beds, comforter covers with a diamond-shaped hole in the middle that only fit

Soviet wool blankets—precious products of a world whose currency was disintegrating. Coarse aluminum pots covered in an enamel glaze, which we later discovered to be highly toxic, stood in the backs of our cupboards. The grammar books terrorized me, and the children's books— nobody read them.

I preferred the stamps to the contents of the parcels. I cut them out, soaked them in water, peeled them from the packages and dried them carefully on our kitchen counter. My parents found Yuri Gagarin's face, or even 1980 Moscow Olympics philatelic propaganda, a jarring sight on our countertops, but I loved coming home to the smiling faces of the toned, muscular athletes and intrepid cosmonauts. I also liked Lenin as a young, pudgy blond boy, standing in a brown militaristic uniform, a red star pinned to his breast and another embroidered on his cap; he looked like the boy I had a crush on at school.

In one of these parcels was a flimsy paperback called *Birds of Our Forests* (*Ptitsy nashikh lesov*) that my grandmother must have sent in the early 1980s, and which I must have flipped through—or not—before setting it aside on my bookshelf. I rediscovered it a few years ago, when my parents embarked on an extensive home renovation. They tasked me with packing up my old bedroom, which still housed all my Soviet picture books. I reread the usual suspects—fairy tales with folksy illustrations, didactic verse with the requisite dreams of incessant hard work for the industrial homeland, including a peculiar story of a young woman whose mother proudly worked as a senior milkmaid on the collective farm. This all seemed in keeping with my grandmother's unquestioning acceptance of Soviet ideology. Ever a perfectionist and a model student, she only began to question her world after emigration. And even then, reluctantly.

But the book about nature surprised me. The primitively illustrated children's book urged the younger generation to explore the great forests of the Soviet Union. There were woodpeckers, ravens, wood grouse, titmice, little owls, woodcocks, kingfishers, hawks—words that would have meant nothing to me as a child. It was a book I don't remember thanking her for. Maybe it was dwarfed by the bottles of Red Moscow perfume she sent, whose scent I tried to inhale in hopes of recognizing my grandmother. When she arrived in Canada in 1987, her fur coat reeked of mothballs, and it turned out she reserved dabbing Red Moscow behind the ears for special occasions. Between the fur, the arresting bleached blonde hair, the Eastern bloc woollens, and the clothes packed in thick plastic bags that had been washed and air-dried, there was little I recognized of the person to whom I'd written so many letters.

Why my grandmother, who believed in the higher gods of symphony halls and ballet performances, and who had no interest in the natural world, chose to send me a book about Russian birds remains a mystery to me. Her experiences with the Soviet natural world were limited to forced summers working on the kolkhoz, where she picked cotton or sugar beets for days on end. "That was enough nature for a lifetime," she told me.

"Why did you buy me this book?" For a moment, I imagined that my grandmother had been the accidental culprit, that the cheap Soviet paperback had been the driving force behind my transformation from nature novice to bona fide bird nerd, that my interest in the avian world wasn't so much a genealogical anomaly as historically determined.

"I bought you dozens of books—at one point, I just bought all the new children's books I could find. Even translations."

"But did you imagine I'd become interested in birds?"

"You know, I don't think I even read the titles." My grandmother refuses to have any involvement in my new bird life. To her it makes little sense. "Normal people go to the opera," she tells me, "but you now go to bed at nine o'clock, set your alarm for four in the morning, and look at birds. *Meshuga*." Craziness, she calls it in Yiddish. My grandmother, who can't speak Yiddish, uses the language whenever she wants to emphasize a point; the language gives her generations' worth of authority. My decision to choose the outdoors baffled my grandmother; hadn't her ancestors, the Lupolover-Lupolansky clan, had their fill of the dirty outdoors in their shtetls in the Pale of Settlement, where Jews had been forced to live since the time of Catherine the Great? Wouldn't they have run toward civilization and chosen institutions of higher learning and the glamour of opera houses and concert halls if only it had been accessible to them? I didn't realize I was disappointing an entire lineage. The outdoors were for other people.

"I still think you must have known," I say.

"I wanted you to speak Russian and love literature, so I sent you poetry by Agniya Barto and Sergei Mikhalkov. I also wanted you to become a scientist, so I sent you my favourite primer of microbes." Poems about disciplined children of good strong Soviet workers, biology for beginners—those books still lay on my shelf, untouched.

"Well, the birds are your fault," I tease her.

"Your grandfather always said the books were useless. 'Who will read them?' he asked me when I forced him to carry boxes to the post office. I told him that maybe you'd become a scientist."

"Birdwatching is related to science."

"The wrong kind of science." She looks at me, her glasses resting on the tip of her nose. I had dashed her dreams of a granddaughter MD who helped fight cancer and replaced them with a granddaughter who went out at dawn every Saturday morning with a pair of binoculars and watched birds.

"Do you at least take photographs?"

"Good camera equipment is too heavy."

"So, what—you just look?"

"It's not just looking. I study the birds. I observe them carefully, and sometimes I write a blog post about what I see. But yes, basically I just look."

"Do people pay you for your blog posts?"

I laugh. Not only is it the wrong kind of science, but it also fails in the realm of practicality. Yet another letdown she has had to endure in old age.

"So, wait, you wake up so early just to look? At least with hunters, I understand. They have something to bring home. But looking?"

I tell her that hunting is how birdwatching actually began. John James Audubon killed all of his specimens before painting them. Before the advent of optics, there was no way to study a bird without shooting it. I tell her all of this, but she's already looking elsewhere. I've disappointed her, and I imagine she's contemplating the one thing she wouldn't dare say: so many years of education, a PhD in comparative literature from Princeton, and now all you can talk about is watching birds?

BUT A FEW WEEKS LATER, SHE CALLED ME.

"Come over quick. I found a book for you in our library. It's filled with many different-coloured birds—probably every single bird in the world."

"What's it called?"

"I'll even steal it, if you want."

"I think you can just borrow it."

"Why borrow? I don't think anybody will miss a book about birds."

Given my grandmother's track record for gifts, I didn't know what to expect.

The book my grandmother stole for me from her apartment building library turned out to be the Golden Field Guide *Birds of North America*, one of the first field guides to go viral before the age of the Internet. Even though much of the nomenclature has changed, I had long coveted this vintage 1966 edition. It occupied a notable place on my growing shelf of bird books that I wasn't yet fully able to decipher.

And Then What?

IT TOOK ME AN ENTIRE YEAR TO MAKE IT OUT BIRDING AGAIN after seeing my first red-winged blackbird. I gasped, I looked, I saw for the first time, and then I retreated. Was I ready to become *that kind of person*? You know, one of *them*? Fashion qualms aside, I didn't even have the vocabulary. I thought back to my first day with the bird group, when everything I said took an infelicitous turn.

"You're the birdwatching group, right?" Why hadn't I just said hi? Obviously, the people with giant birds on their sweatshirts were birdwatchers.

"We're actually birders," said the woman with the red-and-black bird on her sweatshirt, who later introduced herself as Heather.

I nodded, but wasn't that what I had just said? I did a poor job hiding my befuddlement, and when I went home I did some quick Internet research about the taxonomic differences between *birders* and *birdwatchers*. I learned that the latter had a more contemplative bent, whereas the former prided themselves on their obsessive quest. To them, *bird* was both noun and verb. *To bird* meant to actively, sometimes even compulsively, pursue birds, no matter the distance. For a rarity, nowhere was too far to travel. I remembered hearing Brete talk about a spur-of-the-moment trip to get the Eurasian wigeon in Rondeau—I Googled the distance and realized they'd driven a total of 580 kilometres to see a single bird. Now I understood what Heather had meant by *birders*.

I decided then and there, sitting in front of my computer, that there was something suspect about birders. These were people who didn't think twice about jumping into their car at the mere mention of a rarity on one of the birding listservs, who travelled as far as it took to see a new bird. Only, as I quickly learned, instead of "seeing" birds, birders "get" them. That telltale verb puts their experience in the same emotional category as that of hunters, only theirs is a quest without the blood. The entire enterprise began to feel testosterone-driven and senseless to me. I was looking for contemplation, for a meditative pursuit, not a borderline compulsive fixation. I didn't think I wanted to be a *birder*. But something about being a *birdwatcher* felt too passive, borderline geriatric, and I wasn't sure I wanted that either.

I wasn't yet ready to invest in proper optics, and a family friend let me borrow her late husband's binoculars indefinitely. The binoculars belonged to Uncle Slade, the same Uncle Slade who had once politely asked me to leave the room so that he could perform his godfatherly duty; I stood outside the door of his study, fully expecting him to give my best friend, Jessica, a present, something he might not have felt comfortable doing in my presence, but it turned out he had prepared a speech all about the birds and the bees and how during the process of intercourse and subsequent potential impregnation, hundreds of millions of sperm would be vying for Jessica's one illustrious egg. He had rehearsed his speech. I watched my friend emerge from the room, blushing, with Uncle Slade following behind her, a proud smile etched into his face. Slade, the childless, dapper gentleman, who spoke with a British accent, dressed up for dinner and treasured his responsibilities toward his beloved goddaughter.

I didn't find out about Slade's interest in birdwatching until after he'd passed away and his widow offered his binoculars to me, though I might have guessed, since he'd always had a passionate interest in nature. He had once talked me into a stupor about the Precambrian Shield. For the first three years of my foray into birdwatching, whenever I raised Slade's Bausch & Lomb binoculars to my eyes, I inevitably thought of a phalanx of sperm barrelling toward a poor, unsuspecting egg.

FOR A YEAR, THE MALE RED-WINGED BLACKBIRD WAS THE only bird I knew. I saw it everywhere, from early spring well into late fall, and pointed it out to whomever I happened to be with.

"What's the bird next to it?" my husband asked, after I had shown him a red-winged blackbird for the tenth time.

"I have no idea. The red-winged is the only bird I can ID."

"ID?"

"Identify. Birders ID things." I tested out the lingo. Too bad I only had one ID to my name.

"Are you going to meet that group again?"

I shrugged. I had Slade's binoculars, but I wasn't sure. That grebe day still intimidated me. How long would we have to stand on the shore of Lake Ontario admiring ducks that all looked the same? What if I again proudly pointed out a rare mottled brown duck with an eye-stripe and a blue patch on its wing, which turned out to be a female mallard? But it wasn't so much the humiliation that deterred me or the uphill learning battle that I was about to plunge into, but the fact that the hobby felt entirely static. We stood by the lake for a long time, binoculars glued to our eyes, looking out onto the water, calling out IDs, comparing results, questioning plumage, waiting for the moment when we "got" a bird. Wouldn't the novelty wear off after a while? I could imagine getting excited about a bird once, but what happened after the tenth sighting?

And what was the purpose of birding anyhow? Even my hairdresser, Randy, was confused when I described what it meant to "go birding," and he asked in earnest, "So you see a bird and then what?"

"Some people list."

"They what?"

"They keep lists. Like a running life list of all the birds you've ever seen." I didn't tell him about the more compulsive listers who also kept year lists, country lists, province lists, city lists, day lists. "Those people are called listers."

"Is that what you're going to be? Julia the Bird Lister?"

"Not sure."

"But still, you have all these lists, and then what?"

I had no answer for Randy. I wasn't sure what the point of it all was or what I wanted out of the enterprise exactly, but I did know one thing: I had just left behind a goal-oriented life that had clear-cut expectations. I had gone to graduate school and embarked on a coveted tenure-track job teaching Russian literature at a research university in Missouri, a dream job according to my checklist. Absolutely nothing was wrong with the job; my colleagues were lovely and supportive, my students charming and hardworking, and yet when I came home in the evenings to my spacious apartment overlooking the town's picturesque Katy Trail, my only desire was to crack open a beer, and then another, and possibly a third, until I forgot where I was exactly and how I got there, and day would press itself definitively into night. I resigned after three years.

All I knew was that for a whole year, I kept thinking about the red-winged blackbird. *Agelaius phoeniceus*—literally, the red gregarious one. I wondered about its name, since the wings weren't entirely red; there was just a little red patch on the wing, lined with a contour of mustard-yellow against a slick black background. It was a more refined version of the crows I had seen as a child. I had no idea that red-wings were such common birds; each sighting felt like a feat of scientific prowess on my part. For the first time since moving back to Toronto after quitting my job, life felt exhilarating. I could identify something in nature. I was learning to speak a new language.

I BLAME THE RED-WINGED BLACKBIRD FOR EVERYTHING that happened next. It would have been altogether understandable if I'd fallen for a more illustrious species, one that's either difficult to spot or rare for a particular area. But my spark bird—the bird that demarcated a before and after in my life—is a common backyard bird. Red-wings are ubiquitous; even people who claim to know nothing about birds know about red-winged blackbirds.

I think of other late birding bloomers, including Phoebe Snetsinger, one of my birding heroes. She didn't start birding seriously until she was thirty-four years old and a mother of four. Her life shifted into high gear when she saw a Blackburnian warbler in her backyard; this sighting began a lifelong chase of birds, and she was the first person in the world to accumulate a life list of over eight thousand birds. A tiny flittering warbler with a fiery orange throat set off by a black-and-yellow facial mask would make anybody gasp. The exquisite neotropical migrant appears in central and eastern North America in the spring, on its way to breeding grounds in northern Canada, and in the fall, when travelling back to its wintering grounds in Central America. To me, the Blackburnian is a supermodel among warblers, in a class of its own, flashy beyond the realm of the acceptable. Confident and immaculately coiffed, it's a warbler whose body I'd happily inhabit for a few days, if only to know what it might feel like to be that person who makes heads turn.

But the red-winged blackbird, the common backyard bird, made me gasp and wonder. How many other common species had I overlooked while I'd been so busy checking things off a list, waiting for life to *happen to me*?

Deerkill and Other Beginnings

BIRDERS LOVE BEGINNERS. I UNDERSTOOD MY PRIVILEGED position when everybody hovered around me, eager to make sure I got good looks at every single bird we were seeing. Especially that first spring, when I could barely see anything at all.

"What was your favourite bird of the day?" Benito asked over brunch. We'd been birding for three hours straight, most of which was time spent standing still, and I wasn't feeling too gregarious. But I found Benito charming: he spoke English with a South American accent, and I instantly liked this older gentleman who dressed in every possible shade of khaki and who had deliberately developed two competing passions in anticipation of his new retirement identity, post-engineering. If he wasn't birding, he was fishing, and recently he'd also added photography to the mix. I thought of my own grandmother, just a few years older than Benito, also a retired engineer, who now spent most of her time reading, going to the doctor, watching Russian YouTube videos or shopping. For a moment I imagined that hanging out with someone like Benito might do her some good.

"I liked the deerkill."

Benito giggled, and Brete raised his eyes from his omelet, stared at me, then said without a hint of condescension, "That would be killdeer, but yes, it's a lovely early spring migrant."

Ever encouraging, nobody in the group disowned me for mistaking a killdeer for deerkill. I didn't tell them that I fancied the killdeer because I could see it. We caught it walking lazily in a field, and capturing the bird in my binoculars was easy enough. Most of the other birds we saw that day moved at a speed too frantic for my binocular-raising-and-focusing prowess. I also loved the two black ribbons that ran around the bird's neck, because they reminded me of my grandmother's double string of garnet, so dark it looked black.

"I don't think I'm ever going to master the names."

I was feeling deflated, but I noticed that I'd become an instant sensation in the group, not just on account of my age—I was at least thirty years their junior—but because of the challenge I presented. They had never met a beginner who was such a blank slate. My first northern cardinal sent me into raptures of ecstasy and my first hundred blue jays made me shout in wonder. Some people call themselves beginners, but what they really mean is that they have a hard time distinguishing ducks in eclipse plumage. I wasn't one of those. I didn't even know what eclipse plumage was.

"Think of it as learning a new language," Brete said.

If there was one realm I felt comfortable in, it was language learning. Navigating grammatical forms, memorizing vocabulary, deciphering syntax—this brings me joy. But with birding, I was barraged by a language I couldn't make sense of. Throw me in a pool of Romance or Slavic verb forms and I'll find my way, but here, I was completely lost.

I hadn't been a great science student and I barely remembered what orders and families were, let alone how to apply them to birds. I bought *The Sibley Field Guide to Birds of Eastern North America*, which Lucy recommended as the most user-friendly tome. Everybody had been talking about warblers, but when I opened Sibley to the warbler section, I saw two pages packed solid with brownish-greyish-yellowish, virtually identical-looking birds. My eyes started to glaze over. I turned to the beginning of the field guide, hoping I just needed more words in my arsenal to be able to point to the specific parts of the birds that confused me. I stared at a diagram of a bird and digested words like *wing bars*, *eye-rings*, *primaries*, *secondaries* and *greater coverts* until I had to put the field guide away.

It wasn't until three years later that I realized that the two-page spread that had caught my eye featured fall-plumage warblers, which are notoriously difficult. It was like tackling the imperfect subjunctive before you learn the simple past tense: exactly the wrong place for a beginner to start. But I had no idea.

"Start with backyard birds. Once you know your common birds, you'll be able to figure out many of the more challenging ones," Brete said, as we walked along a woodsy path.

"But I don't even have a backyard." How would I ever figure out which ones are the common ones when they all look and sound exotic to me?

"Good point, but it's an expression." First lesson. *Backyard birds* was a euphemism for *common birds*. A backyard bird in Toronto is not the same as a backyard bird in Edmonton. It turns out there is nothing more place-based than birding.

"So what's common here?"

"Well, it depends a bit on the season. Your favourite red-winged blackbird, for one, blue jays, grackles, cardinals, nuthatches, downy woodpeckers." It turned out that Toronto is home to approximately 350 bird species, which meant I had 349 new ones to learn.

"I lost you after red-winged blackbird. But, wait, Toronto has woodpeckers?"

And within minutes, as if on command, a downy appeared and started drumming on a tree at eye level, and I stood there mesmerized. Here was a bird no larger than my hand drumming so vigorously that I worried its head would pop off.

"Being a bird is not for the faint of heart. I'd break my neck if I banged my head against the tree so hard."

"That's probably why you're not a bird," said Brete. And he launched into an explanation of how extra musculature in their skulls means that woodpeckers basically wear an internal bike helmet around their brains and can thump their heads as much as they want without maiming themselves. But even so, I couldn't help anthropomorphizing.

When I was a child and daydreamed about animals, which wasn't that often because I preferred daydreaming about happy marriage plots, I always imagined them at school, sitting at a desk similar to mine, studying for tests and eagerly thinking about what they'd study at university. I had consumed so many novels, superimposing myself on all their characters and ethical dilemmas, that it was the only way I could process the world.

The beauty of birding as a beginner is that everything feels spectacular. I'd never seen anything as blue as the indigo bunting, which looked like it had been dipped in a tub of shiny royal blue paint; depending on the intensity of the light, it sometimes sparkled.

I would pay good money to rewind time to my first encounter with the hooded merganser—my gateway drug to waterfowl. I had thought that a duck was a duck was a duck until I saw this peculiar specimen with a *chevelure* that rivalled that of Louis XIV in stature: a black crest outlining an enormous white patch, all of which fanned out majestically when the duck floated on water. The name didn't do the bird justice; it wasn't just a hood—it was an artistic masterpiece.

"I used to think that ducks all looked the same. This hooded merganser duck is the most beautiful thing I've ever seen."

"It's just a hooded merganser. Not hooded merganser duck."

"Oh."

"Wait until you see a harlequin duck," Heather nearly shouted. When she got excited about a bird, her voice rose in pitch. This retired nurse, who had no shortage of strong feelings about waterfowl, never wore a T-shirt or sweatshirt without a bird on it, which I found odd until I noticed that I'd started aspiring to the same.

I didn't need a harlequin right then. I was happy just staring at the duck in front of me.

"I think I see something interesting—there's a brownish duck behind it with a strange comb-over!"

"That's the female."

"How drab. That's disappointing."

"Welcome to the bird world."

It would take me years to recognize the female species of most birds and not shout out a rarity. Indeed, they were disappointing when compared with their flamboyant male counterparts. But this, it turns out, is an ingenious evolutionary feat: the male's more colourful demeanour attracts female mates, but the female's drabness serves to protect them from predators while they rear their young.

The first time I saw a hooded merganser, which later went by the name of "hoodie" or "hooded merg," I had no trouble picking him out because he was the only one in the pond, with his uninspiring mate following closely behind him. The next time I saw him, he was in a flotilla of ducks, a bunch of dark blobs in the distance, and I was entirely lost. I couldn't make out a single one.

"Where's that stellar crest?"

"Look for shapes as you scan, it'll be easier. When there's no wind, the crest falls flat."

"I guess he forgot to use a blow-dryer."

I finally found him, with the help of Brete's ID skills, but I was completely lost when I heard Heather and Lucy shout out the litany of ducks: common goldeneye, gadwall, long-tailed duck, bufflehead, redhead, ring-necked duck, white-winged scoter, red-breasted merganser, northern shoveler. If someone had told me then that it would take me five years to comfortably ID all those ducks, I would have quit on the spot.

LATER THAT FIRST SPRING, I MET BRETE'S GROUP AT 5:15 A.M. in a high school parking lot in Mississauga.

"Just wait until you see all the warblers," Lucy said. At the mere mention of warblers, her voice quivered with excitement. Even before sunrise, Lucy managed to look elegant, her hair curled and brushed under, exactly the way I tried and failed to style mine, her eye makeup and lipstick delicately applied. She'd been anticipating these warblers all week long.

"What's going to happen?"

"You'll understand why we live for May," Heather chimed in. The bright colours, coupled with the challenge of seeing and ID'ing the warblers during their brief four-week stint in southern Ontario, made their pursuit intoxicating.

I had prepared for this moment by studying Sibley and attempting to memorize the twenty-five or so warblers commonly seen in southern Ontario. Some were easy, with fiery orange necks, but others, like the Tennessee, orange-crowned and Nashville, looked annoyingly similar: greyish, olive hues, with a hint of yellow somewhere. I knew, from reading the field guide and talking to my bird group, that warblers move quickly, but what everybody neglected to tell me was that for my first dozen times looking for warblers, I'd basically be looking at leaves.

My first look at warblers in the field would require binocular technical skill akin to playing a rapid-fire Chopin étude, whereas I was still at the Clementi sonatina level. I could grasp the contours of a bird—barely—when it perched on a (preferably leafless) branch, screaming *take my photo, now!* Nuthatches, chickadees, cedar waxwings and even the elusive evening grosbeak co-operated, and I could see them because they sat still while I fumbled with my focus and raised my binoculars repeatedly until I managed to get them in my view. But warblers never sat still; they flitted about restlessly, often performing aerial flycatching routines.

I thought I knew how to see. In fact, I never questioned my capacity to see because I wore my glasses diligently and so far had managed to pass every eye test. But when I had to locate a warbler with my binoculars, I suddenly lacked the skill to perform the simplest task. I lifted my binoculars and pointed them toward the bird in question, but instead of the mythical black-throated blue warbler Brete had called out, all I could detect was a jiggling leaf, shimmying lazily in the air.

Another thing Brete neglected to mention: my neck would hurt for days, and my first full day of birding would send me straight to my massage therapist for an emergency treatment. Called "warbler neck" for a reason, the condition resulted from staring up in a vertical line while attempting to harness all your intellectual faculties to discern the details of the fluttering bird—wing bars, undertail feathers, facial marking—and match them to the description in the Sibley guide. The neck strain was real, and though my massage therapist didn't admit it, I sensed that my new hobby delighted her.

WHEN YOU'RE OUT IN THE FIELD, THERE'S NOTHING MORE exciting than showing someone a new bird and reliving the experience of seeing it for the first time. I am forever jealous of anybody who has yet to read *Anna Karenina* for the first time, experiencing the thrill of reading Kitty and Levin's unbelievable courtship scene or of watching Levin plough the fields and feel that time has stopped.

After I'd been birding for five years, I took my mom out to Ashbridges Bay and brought my binoculars along, to show her the common ducks for the first time. It was a particularly slow day, too calm to warrant any exciting visitors, and I quickly scanned the water, counting a few red-breasted mergansers with their spiky, Edward Scissorhands–hairdos, and a half-dozen long-tailed ducks. And then I saw a lone male bufflehead directly in front of us. The sun shone right on him, his black and white head suddenly iridescent with shades of green and purple. I handed the binoculars to my mom because I knew the bird would be easy to see; he was in some kind of meditative trance and wasn't diving.

"Look at that black-and-white duck, find it with your naked eye and then point the binoculars at it," I instructed my mother.

"A naked eye?"

"That's what we say when you look without binoculars." I had said it in Russian and it sounded just as ridiculous as in English.

"I can only see water. But it's so beautiful and blue!"

"Good start. Now move your head to the right a little and you should see a duck."

"I can't see anything," my mother said, already frustrated and pointing my binoculars at the sky.

"Try again. Look first, then put the binoculars on it."

"Henri said I might need bifocals but I don't want to go there. This probably isn't good for my eyes, this intense looking. I have special glasses now for seeing things up close. Maybe I should have worn them."

"Just focus! It's right in front of you."

"I can't...oh wait, there's a little black-and-white duck! His head looks purple in the light! Wait, he's looking at me!" I wanted to show my mom a few other birds, but she wasn't interested. She couldn't take her eyes off the bufflehead, which she alternately called buffalo, buffhead, buffleduck—until I stopped correcting her because I realized she had no interest in learning the correct name.

"I didn't know ducks could be so beautiful," she said, the minute we got home and my dad asked where we'd been. And before I had time to get a word in, my mom described the buffalo-duck in perfect detail. "Yulechka is the best bird guide. She knows so much about ducks."

And although I knew that the words meant little—I had spoken them myself on a dozen different occasions, to people who weren't proficient birders but who had shown me something spectacular for the first time—they still felt good.

After seeing the bufflehead, my mother began watching the birds in her backyard. She occasionally gets bored with seeing the same house sparrows, blue jays, American robins and northern cardinals and craves something more exotic. She called me recently to announce a rare bird that had hovered over their roses earlier that day.

"You wouldn't believe what I just saw! It was a multi-coloured bird. The most beautiful thing! What could it be?"

"What colours did you see?"

"Every colour of the rainbow." I couldn't think of a single Ontario bird that matched her description.

"Are you sure it had that many colours?"

"Of course I'm sure. It must have been one of your rare birds. A rainbow bird!" my mother said, content with her new taxonomic discovery. I contemplated telling my mother that the only bird that crossed my mind for a split second was the painted bunting, but if she really had one in her backyard, there would already be three hundred birders looking at it.

Just then, my father interrupted her. "Don't you remember? It was a butterfly, not a bird."

Intraspecific Variability

THE SECOND TIME I GOT MARRIED, THERE WAS NO CAKE. I couldn't face a repeat of my first wedding, when my father tripped on his way to the front door and let out a faint squeal as my three-tiered marzipan-covered lemon wedding cake, in slow motion, escaped his grip, slid off its platform and plummeted, left side first, into the grass. When I opened the door, my father's guilty eyes peered at me from behind the lopsided cake, whose side had now acquired a permanent dusting of twigs.

Instead of interpreting the mangled wedding cake as a questionable omen, I had read it as a sign of exquisite luck. This was exactly the anti-wedding I'd been hoping for. A black dress, no formal invitations, a ceremony at city hall on St. Patrick's Day—a date I chose only because it fit with my graduate school vacation calendar—and a party at my parents' house the next day. And now, a toppled wedding cake cemented our union, which so obviously defied convention.

I married my first husband when I was under the spell of graduate school, as everybody I knew had paired off and

I assumed that nuptials secured a sure path to bona fide adulthood. A visiting French graduate student in philosophy, he astounded me with his encyclopedic knowledge and his passion for comparative mythology. We fell in love with our respective bookshelves and envisioned a future of merged multilingual libraries. Smugly, I mocked my friends and thought our love was stronger, more authentic, more lasting than theirs. In the end, I married a person of my own creation.

There was nothing original about our breakup. It included all the hallmarks of a disintegrating marriage—deceit, betrayal, frustrated expectations. Until the final moments of crumbling, we hadn't even really argued. As things collapsed definitively, I remembered the cake.

THE SECOND TIME AROUND, THERE WOULD BE NO THREE-tiered cake. I didn't want to provide us with an easy omen, with a sure sign in retrospect. We married on Leon's lunch break, since he worked two blocks from city hall, and a third of our fifteen-person wedding party came uninvited. I barely knew the five officemates sitting in the second row, who needed proof that this forty-six-year-old poster child for eternal bachelorhood was indeed getting married. If I were to break up with Leon, I thought to myself at our wedding, I wouldn't be able to trace it back to this simple, impersonal twenty-minute ceremony; we would be worthy of a more complicated narrative. In my repertory of modes of leaving, I had already mastered the surreptitious departure, the protracted disintegration, the explosive combustion, the electric jolt of mutual horror, the non-negotiable betrayal, the irredeemable disenchantment and, perhaps worst of all, the transformation of love into pity. Our breakup, if it were to happen, would have to follow an altogether different trajectory, I decided.

But I worried. I worried that we weren't compatible enough (he didn't like classical music as much as I'd hoped), I worried that we wouldn't survive the three-year mark (not one of my previous relationships had made it past three years), I worried that we'd run out of things to say to one another and that our aesthetic tastes would turn out to be irreconcilable. Most of all, I worried that someone who had gotten divorced barely three years after her father dropped her wedding cake on the ground might have been, somewhere deep down, cursed by the evil eye.

Five months into our marriage, I discovered birds. Two years into our marriage, I became the proud owner of a sewage lagoon permit, which enabled me to enter the Brighton sewage treatment plant at my own risk, with pants tucked into socks, and marvel at shorebirds and other assorted waterfowl. Ten years into our marriage, I haven't yet acquired a multipocketed vest, but watching fellow birders parade theirs with pride, I know it's only a matter of time before I start researching brands myself.

"You weren't like this when I married you" is a refrain my husband likes to utter, jokingly. Or maybe not so jokingly. But it's true. I wasn't like this when I married him. And neither was he.

LOVE, AS WE KNOW IT, RARELY FIGURES INTO THE AVIAN equation. Polygamy and polyandry prevail in their world, usually in the service of Darwinian survival. Monogamous birds are few and far between—puffins are a famed example—but most birds are biologically wired to allow for multiple partners: DNA analysis of eggs has revealed that there can be numerous fathers within a single clutch, which means that the female's body is created to allow for the storage of sperm from different partners to fertilize the eggs.

Bird sex is lightning quick, with the very rare exception, and theirs cannot be judged by human standards of pleasure and fidelity, comfort and security. I once came upon two peregrine falcons flirting in mid-air above a quarry just north of Hamilton. I quickly raised my binoculars and watched them engage in a rapturous amorous chase and quickly copulate on a utility pole, all of which lasted no longer than twenty seconds. Afterwards, the diminutive male flew off, looking self-satisfied, and the more robust female rustled her feathers, looked around ravenously and went about her business.

Birding didn't teach me how to fall in love. Besides, I was already an expert in that, especially falling in love with the variety of human who was wrong for me in every way; my roster of failed relationships held specimens of whom I was ashamed, whom I wished I could press the fast-forward button on, and also fellows who might have been right for me had I met them at a different stage of life—but birding taught me how to *stay* in love, an exercise at which I had desperately needed coaching. My husband and I met the old-fashioned way, introduced by my then-eighty-nine-year-old grandmother. Her neighbour had a good friend who had a son who was single; my grandmother was dissatisfied with every guy I picked out for myself. After a brief discussion and a quick photo exchange, the two of them decided that this was worth a shot. "He goes to the film festival regularly," my grandmother told me. His greatest selling point, once she remembered I loved movies. "And the ballet." What she didn't tell me was that he had season tickets to the National Ballet of Canada and attended performances with his mother.

I went on the date partly out of desperation and in no small part out of curiosity. Who was this Russian-Jewish computer programmer who also liked movies and ballet? It turned out he was also an amateur powerlifter who could easily deadlift the weight of my entire nuclear family. I stared at his bulky chest and arms, entirely unable to imagine how we could negotiate any kind of intimate scenario. Would he crush me? (The answer turned out to be no.)

I unexpectedly fell in love with Leon, largely because he was nothing like me. I had usually chosen partners based on shared interests or similarities. I needed to be able to see myself in the person, to recognize quirks and insecurities in order to feel a certain comfort. Here, the shared interests were minimal, though we both liked going for walks and finding good coffee shops and wandering aimlessly, and what appealed to me was in fact that he was nothing like me, that I couldn't recognize myself in any part of him. Here was a man who didn't have anxiety about finding the right word, the right sentence to describe a thought, who never worried about the rhythm of a phrase—although I later learned that he worried every bit as much about the elegance of his lines of code, and that he too embarked on a form of writing every time he was faced with a work problem. We read different books entirely—his were sci-fi and fantasy, all the same size, all perfectly ordered, whereas I was a child of realist novels, completely uninterested in other worlds. Unexpectedly, he made me laugh, didn't find faults in my physical appearance, didn't judge me, and just let me be.

THE FIRST FIFTY TIMES I SAW A WHITE-BREASTED NUTHATCH, I confused it with a black-capped chickadee. Both had black heads and similarly sized grey backs, and both hung out in the same trees. It wasn't until later that I learned that their behaviour differs completely—the nuthatch creeps down a tree headfirst, its bill longer and pointier, its eye-stripe prominent. I didn't see these details immediately—it took months for them to imprint on my mind, but once I learned to recognize them, the two birds seemed forever different to me.

Birding is about discerning differences, sometimes minute—a blackpoll and a bay-breasted warbler are indistinguishable in fall plumage, except for the colour of their feet. (The blackpoll's are yellowish.) Even though I rarely manage to distinguish them in the field, I now know that if only they'd stay still for long enough, which warblers so rarely do, I could.

By the time Leon and I had our first serious argument, I had already spent time in the field with a scope, puzzling through the differences between a greater and lesser scaup, though it would take years to learn that the lesser was the one with the slightly elongated head and the greenish or purplish iridescence, which is only visible in perfect sunlight. The differences between species were subtle, but unmistakable once one grasped the details of their morphology. Maybe that was just it: we didn't both have to be a greater scaup.

The more I watched birds, the more I learned to appreciate the inter-species differences between my husband and me. We were clearly part of the same genus but belonged to different species. So what if Leon refused to see *Tosca* with me? So what if the symphony left him cold? I stopped trying to convert him to my interests. I began to think about our differences in perspective, like the varied bird species that I was learning to discern. They all coexist and their beauty, to me, lies precisely in their distinct characteristics.

THERE'S A SPONTANEITY THAT COMES WITH BIRDING. THE bird you're looking for often isn't the one that appears, no matter how well you plan for it and how many listservs you dutifully consult. And the one that appears is often more surprising and just as great as, if not better than, the one you're looking for. In my quest to find my first red-headed woodpecker, we came across a merlin sitting on a branch directly across the street from us, giving us perfect looks, posing for the camera, more still than I'd ever seen one perch. I was so focused on seeing my woodpecker that I didn't pay enough attention to the merlin and didn't realize how rare his posture was, didn't realize that I might never see a merlin this close up again.

If I could have that day back, I would correct my disinterest in the merlin. I was so obsessed with my woodpecker that I ignored the merlin because I hadn't planned for it. It wasn't my target bird and I couldn't muster enough enthusiasm. It's been four years since that day, and I'm still trying to get that good a look at a merlin. I've seen many red-headed woodpeckers since then, but never another merlin that close, that co-operative, that picture-perfect.

I didn't learn the lesson that day, because I was so focused on my reward—finally seeing a red-headed woodpecker—but I learned it a while later: focus on what's in front of you, on what you're looking at rather than what you want to see. I try to apply that to my marriage. Focus on what's there right now.

It turned out that when I didn't look into the future, when I stopped practising the art of augury, when I didn't try to obsessively plan out our life, the present was actually exactly as I wanted.

The Migratory Urge

IN 1797, JOHANN ANDREAS NAUMANN COINED THE TERM *Zugunruhe* to describe migratory restlessness. At the time, medieval myths about migration still circulated; there was a need to discount ideas that swallows and swifts hibernated or, better yet, spent half the year underwater. For about a century before Naumann's research, natural scientists would put birds in cages to determine whether their instinct to migrate was in fact innate. They observed a curious phenomenon: every spring and fall, the birds became highly agitated, hopped forwards and back, moved about anxiously, and tried to fly on the spot as best they could. This behaviour lasted for about thirty days—the usual duration of migratory flights—and began about an hour before sunset, the precise time when birds usually set out for their nocturnal journeys. In the fall, caged migrants even accumulated girth, the weight gain that would help them prepare for their long journey south.

Naumann realized that not only did birds need to migrate, but their DNA dictated the course of their migratory path. The goals of migration are simple: food and reproduction. Once seasonal resources are exhausted and the urge to breed surges, they hop on the flight path northward. After breeding has successfully taken place, they plump up and journey southward. Their perilous path is inscribed in their internal hardwiring, and each spring they breed in the exact same territory they've known for generations.

The very idea of *Zugunruhe* felt antithetical to my pursuit of a home. Once a home becomes comfortable, biological imperative sends one back to another, equally essential, place. But how could it possibly be home if one's genetic makeup forces one to abandon it as soon as seasonal resources are exhausted? How can it be that home is the shuttling back and forth between the two?

I COME FROM A LONG LINE OF MIGRANTS. OURS WAS NOT A seasonal affair, but rather was dictated by geopolitical imperative. First pogroms, then World War II, caused my grandparents on both sides to flee largely Jewish-populated towns in Ukraine. My father's family took refuge in Siberia and my mother's was evacuated to Uzbekistan. My grandmother returned to Odessa in 1944, at the age of thirteen, only to find that their apartment no longer belonged to them and all their possessions had been stolen by the neighbours.

"I saw my upstairs neighbour reading my copy of André Gide's *Counterfeiters* and using our dresser. Eventually we got the dresser back, but not my novel," my grandmother told me. It was only later that I learned that the name in her passport—Nusya—is a short form for her real name, Anna. Inscribed in an official document by a drunk civil servant whom her mother didn't have the money to bribe, she'd even been cheated of her real name.

It took years for them to find a place to live, acquire furniture and resume their life. The evacuation years robbed my grandmother of her chance to become a musician and dictated the course of her life afterwards. She ended up studying metallurgical engineering not out of any fascination with metals and alloys, but because it was the only department offering scholarships to Jewish students. Her second choice after music would have been medicine, but the university in Odessa had strict quotas for Jews—less than 5 per cent—and she didn't even have the heart to apply. Forced migration had radically altered her life.

"Do you know what it feels like to work for thirty years in a job you hate?" my grandmother asked me when I complained about having too much to do. She couldn't stand her job, counted down the days until she turned fifty-five and would be able to retire. But life had something else in store for her: her only daughter, only son-in-law and only granddaughter received exit visas to Israel and decided to emigrate in 1978. Whether it was on account of the forced evacuation and the subsequent difficulties of remaking a life, which came at the cost of all her dreams, or the more prosaic fact that she had believed Soviet 1970s propaganda, which painted the capitalist West as a debauched and destitute hell, my grandparents refused to apply for visas with us. Instead, they tried to bribe my parents with an apartment in Petrozavodsk, where my father worked as an adjunct professor of piano. My grandmother had no idea that her adamant refusal to apply for visas would result in a nine-year separation from her only child, during which time she'd be widowed at the age of fifty-four.

We emigrated anyhow, travelling by train from Kharkov, via Poland, to Vienna, where we arrived with twenty suitcases filled with books, Soviet tool kits, flashlights and bedding, and so heavy that we couldn't even move them. My parents' last memory of my grandfather is seeing him running, breathless, after our slowly departing train, trying to hand over the last of his money to my dad through the open window. He wouldn't live to see his daughter in her new home.

As a child, my only memory of my grandmother came from a family photograph where she sits, stern and unsmiling, with a fierce look in her eyes and hands crossed just below her chest. When I met her again, nine years later, I was afraid to approach her. She arrived with suitcases bursting with Bulgarian dresses, East German sweaters, Estonian undergarments—the best clothes the crumbling Soviet Union had to offer. I later found out that all of her clothes had been purchased at least five to ten years prior— all of them in pristine condition, never worn, awaiting a life in the West that was about to begin.

She scowled the night she arrived in Canada, and had I known why, I would have buried my head in her naphthalene-scented coat and cried for everything she had lost. She hadn't had a reason to smile in that photo, either—it had been taken on the eve of our departure: my grandmother, whose migratory path had deprived her of the life she wanted, was about to lose her only child and grandchild to a flight path of a different nature.

WHILE WE STILL LIVED IN THE SOVIET UNION, I GAINED migratory experience. Born in Kharkov, where my father's family lived and had connections with a good, if bribed, obstetrician, I shuttled between there and Leningrad, where my mother was in her second year at the conservatory, and

Odessa, where my grandparents lived. When I was two, my father worked in Petrozavodsk, on Lake Onega, north of Leningrad, and I travelled there as well, infrequently, and probably added even more chaos to the already squalid communal apartment living quarters that housed both students and junior faculty members. It wasn't until I reached graduate school that I doubled the mileage flown in the first three years of my life.

I was three and a half when we left the country passportless—a punishment mandated by the Soviet state for abandoning one's homeland. Our departure offered no possibility of return. In Vienna, our interim émigré passports had the word *Staatenlos* written in the place of our nationalities: Stateless. Nationless. Pressed into the crisp yellow pages of our passports, the typewriter-inscribed letters, all upper-case. A bureaucratically accepted term for *homeless*.

Our year in Vienna was a migratory stopover, only we differed from warblers in that we had no idea where exactly we would end up. Unlike the Prothonotary warbler that breeds in the same trees every spring, we shuttled back and forth between five embassies accepting Russian-Jewish refugees in the late 1970s. Our choices were Germany, Australia, New Zealand, Canada and the United States. We had diverted from our intended path, which would have brought us to Israel, because my father's age meant he could still have been drafted to serve in the army. Countries in the southern hemisphere felt too removed from civilization, even for my intrepid parents, so they decided not to apply to Australia and New Zealand. In my alternative history fantasies, I always wonder what would have happened had we immigrated to Auckland; would I have taken one look at a kiwi and become a birder sooner? Would I have discovered natural history instead of literature?

My parents' first choice of destination was Germany, since they had both studied the language in school and knew that the country was particularly hospitable to musicians. The plan to move to Germany wasn't a bad one, but it didn't account for one detail: my dad's cousin from Edmonton happened to be on sabbatical the year of our migratory stopover in Vienna. He visited us, and though they communicated largely in hand gestures, broken Yiddish and snippets of Russian, by the end of three days in Vienna he had accomplished his mission. We would be immigrating to Edmonton.

"*Pochemu* Germany? How can you go to Germany?"

"Piano. Muzika. Culture."

"But Jews? In Germany?"

And those two words—Jews, Germany—were enough for my parents to rethink their decision. They knew what it meant to feel Jewish in an inhospitable climate. My father couldn't escape his Jewish roots no matter how much he tried; he carried his father's name inside the middle name that all Russians have—his patronymic, Moyseevich—which instantly gave away his religion. My mother had been discouraged from applying to graduate school because the fifth line of her passport, the dreaded line that revealed your nationality, had the word "Jewish" printed in upper-case letters. The tricky thing about being Jewish in the Soviet Union was that it was considered both a religion and a nationality, which branded a person for life. No matter the fact that my grandmother had forced my grandfather to change his name from Itzik to Grigoriy so that my mother would endure life with a more palatable patronymic—it didn't make an ounce of difference. Inna Grigorievna would always be Jewish in Soviet Russia. And the idea of being a Jew in Germany suddenly struck my parents as even worse than everything they had already endured.

Vienna turned out to be a stopover as nourishing and restful as any songbird could dream of. While waiting for bureaucratic procedures of a migratory flight-path diversion to Canada, my parents enjoyed a year without having to work. They bought cheap standing-room tickets for the Vienna State Opera (my mother stood through *The Ring* on four-inch heels) and the Musikverein, and spent time in museums that had pay-what-you-can days. They lived off food stamps and vouchers, and shared a bedroom with their three-year-old daughter—and still my parents think back to their Viennese interlude as their first exhilarating taste of freedom. They were resting up and gaining strength for an immigration that would transform them into workhorses for the next two decades of their lives.

We weren't eager to leave Vienna, but legally we couldn't stay, and life as *Staatenlos* nomads couldn't go on indefinitely either. My parents had abandoned one home and had no choice but to make another.

IT HAPPENS THAT MIGRANTS ARE SOMETIMES BLOWN OFF course or they get confused and do a bit of reverse migration before reaching their destination. I saw this once at Point Pelee, in southwestern Ontario, site of Canada's greatest migratory spectacle: standing at the tip of the peninsula, I could see confused scarlet tanagers flying south instead of north, disoriented and lost. The year we spent in Edmonton resembled a form of reverse migration; my parents had to learn a new language, adjust to a new world, work seven days a week and plan their move to somewhere with a more hospitable climate, both meteorological and cultural.

Meanwhile, I learned to read and write in English and began disappearing into books. Facing the wall next to my bed, I read late into the evening without anybody noticing, because one of my parents taught piano students in my bedroom, while the other worked in the living room.

We moved to Vancouver in search of better musical opportunities and greater distance from our well-meaning relatives, who still wondered why my parents hadn't taken jobs at the Army & Navy Store immediately upon arriving in Canada. They had never met concert pianists before and considered music a great pastime for evenings and weekends. My aunties who lived across the street couldn't help commenting on how my mother dressed me and pointing out that if only my parents were more organized, I wouldn't have to make the school-bus driver wait every morning. In Vancouver, I learned French, and when given the chance to go on nature walks, I opted to stay home and read and dream of being elsewhere. Even when my parents sent me to kibbutz-style overnight camp, I retreated to the nurse's office every time we had a strenuous outdoor activity, feigning a stomach ache, so I could write letters to various family members, with detailed explanations of my natural surroundings and all the outdoor activities I could have done but chose not to.

For seven years, we lived in Vancouver and waited. I remember the hope that someday soon, I would have grandparents who lived in the same city as me, who would pick me up from swimming lessons and help me with my math homework.

"They're engineers. They know everything about math," my mother said. Subtracting fractions seemed to be beyond both of our abilities.

"Why can't you help me?"

"I stopped taking math in Grade 8."

"I'm only in Grade 3."

"Even before I stopped taking math, my parents did my homework for me."

I looked at my father and he nodded in agreement. I guess he too had forgotten the ins and outs of fractions. I would just have to wait for my grandparents to arrive to be a straight-A student in math.

By the mid-1980s, I had started telling my friends that my grandparents were refuseniks, even though I didn't quite understand the word. They had been denied exit visas to leave the Soviet Union on account of allegedly being privy to state secrets. But what kinds of secrets could two metallurgical engineers possibly know? Immediately after we emigrated, my mother was branded an enemy of the state, and both my grandparents lost their jobs. We waited. My mother joined a group of activists who fought on behalf of Soviet-Jewish refuseniks. She attended meetings, met famous lawyers from Ottawa, and went on a hunger strike to petition authorities in the Soviet embassy to send a message to KGB officials in Odessa in charge of my grandparents' dossier. Occasionally relatives of other refuseniks came to stay with us. Names such as *Anatoly Sharansky*, *Ida Nudel* and *Alexander Lerner* floated through our house and I studied their biographies; they'd been incarcerated in work camps in Siberia for attempting to defect from the Soviet Union. I imagined that when my grandparents got out of Russia, someone would write a book about them, too, complete with black-and-white photographs and maybe a mention of their granddaughter waiting for them in Vancouver, her math homework spread out on the kitchen table.

The arrival wasn't what I had been expecting. About twenty people from the Vancouver branch of the Soviet Jewry Committee came with flowers and danced the hora in the airport; it made the front page of the *Vancouver Sun*, but nobody at school talked about it the next day. Their flight from that country which nobody leaves freely was of little concern to my friends and teachers. The fact that my grandmother arrived with my great-grandmother, and without her husband, interested nobody. That my grandfather had died the previous year of cancer—long before people battled the disease with courage, his illness simply felled him, definitively, between one telegram, stating metastases in the liver, and the next, two months later, announcing his death—was a private tragedy in our house, borne by my mother alone.

VANCOUVER WOULD RESURFACE IN MY PEREGRINATIONS when I returned to attempt to make a home for myself after my undergrad degree, with a boyfriend I'd known since childhood. I had migrated back to my familiar surroundings, and everywhere I went, I searched for remnants of my life there as a child. Nothing was as my nostalgia remembered it; our old house had been painted, the fence my parents worked hard to afford had been removed. I was more invested in my past life in Vancouver than my present one, but my boyfriend couldn't understand where I was coming from; he had no idea about migratory restlessness. Our apartment with a stunning view of False Creek should have felt like home but didn't, and I morphed into an evening-class enthusiast: I tried my hand at pottery, Italian conversation classes and aerobics, all the while dreaming of elsewhere.

We were young. We lacked the capacity to talk to one another without scalding with our criticism and unhappiness. I couldn't tell him that I was starting to feel like a caged migrant; instead, while I worked a series of odd jobs, I applied to graduate school, and at the end of that trial year, which I had hoped would hold the key to my future, I packed my belongings and returned to the east coast, my face still smarting from the nightly tears and ossified circular conversations. We blamed one another for our shattered dreams, but if I'd only known about the biological imperative of avian migration, I'd have been able to tell him what I was feeling. That I couldn't stay, that this couldn't be my end point, that the nourishment here was insufficient, that home would have to be elsewhere.

NO MATTER HOW MUCH I LOVE THE MONTH OF MAY IN Toronto, when I see black-throated blue warblers daily, their black face masks set off by metallic navy head and black and white underbelly, I know it's short-lived. They cannot stay for long; their route has been predetermined. To stop a black-throated blue from migrating is to kill it. I wish I could stretch out the contours of May, and I do, in my own way, by waking up at dawn and birding as much as humanly possible. I know that birds are only at their brightest for a short time—to attract the best mate possible. The colours are at their most vibrant. And just as I'm getting to know them, as I get used to them, fall in love with them, they're off. My consolation is that they'll be back next year. And the year after that.

I couldn't work through anything in Vancouver because I had to be elsewhere. Instead, my mother's friend, who owned a furniture company, helped me pack up all my books and shipped them back to my parents' house in Toronto for me.

I had left Toronto in 1993 as an eighteen-year-old, convinced the city was provincial, boring, not where I wanted to be. And yet no matter where I was, it called to me.

MIGRATORY DISTANCES VARY WIDELY AMONG SPECIES; SOME birds, like the Arctic tern, fly great distances so that they might live exclusively in daylight. They breed in the High Arctic in the summer and traverse the world to winter near the South Pole. The bird spends approximately half the year in flight, migrating between poles and covering a distance of 47,000 kilometres a year. To be constantly in motion—that's their home. Sometimes I imagine myself as an Arctic tern, forever thirsty for light.

"Wouldn't things be great if we moved to the Yukon?" I asked Leon.

"You're afraid of large animals." True. I remembered hiking around Kathleen Lake, in Kluane National Park and Reserve, petrified that I'd be attacked by a bear. I asked every hiker we passed whether they'd seen bears that day. Finally, I had to ask an Austrian couple in broken German, and they gave me that look that basically said we-leave-the-city-precisely-to-escape-people-like-you. It turned out they were there in the hope of running into large wildlife. When we drove the empty highways, I put Leon on moose-alert and forbade him to fall asleep.

"I could go to bravery school."

"Where would you take your ballet class?"

"Good point."

"Or go to the opera?"

I couldn't argue. For now, Yukon was off the table. Not on account of the long winters, which I felt would suit me, but on account of my dire fear of four-legged creatures and my particularly urban cultural appetites.

A FEW YEARS AGO, ON A BIRDING TRIP, WE STOPPED AT A nineteenth-century estate in Haldimand County called Ruthven, a reliable place for eastern bluebirds and tufted titmouse sightings. When we arrived, the small bird banding station was open, and before I knew it, I was handed a tufted titmouse to hold and release. I protested and the master bander looked at me and said, "Are you really scared of a bird?" I took the bird in my hand reluctantly, afraid to hurt it. And there I was, me—the person who's afraid of most living creatures, who had never had pets, who as a child was told that if you approach a dog it will likely bite you, the person who feared she was incapable of handling any animal without maiming it—shaking slightly, but holding a bird in my hand. Someone at the banding station immortalized the moment in a photograph, and in it I am smiling nervously, my grip on the bird with an energetic grey tuft a bit too intense. Or perhaps I'm smiling because I was feeling a bird's heartbeat in my hand for the first time.

And as I let it go, its spindly legs lifting off my outstretched palm, I wanted to follow the bird's trajectory. So this is what it means to be on the wing, to take flight, I thought.

A year later, I applied to volunteer at the migration monitoring station in Toronto, and for four months of the year, I am still privy to the pull of migration. Holding a five-gram golden-crowned kinglet in my hand before releasing it, it's as if I too, in that moment, were on a flight path.

LBJS

WHERE I COME FROM, THE CBC MEANS PRECISELY ONE THING: the Canadian Broadcasting Corporation, our federally funded source of news, music and sundry cultural inspiration. But in the bird world, it means something entirely different. It's the Christmas Bird Count, a citizen-science-cum-social event, where birders from across North America tally up all the birds seen on a particular day in a specific area in order to then pool data to detect changes in bird populations over time. What it means to me, more specifically, is that I have an excuse to go out birding, no matter the weather. It's also a lesson in the importance of counting.

The Christmas Bird Count began in 1900 when ornithologist Frank Chapman suggested that people count birds rather than hunt them. The count came out of the "Side Hunt," a tradition where hunters would go out into the woods and whoever returned with the largest number of feathered trophies won. Chapman proposed a Christmas Bird Census without guns, and we've been practising it ever since.

I signed up for my first CBC out of curiosity. What could be more absurd than counting not only every single species you see, but every individual among the species? A thankless task that also felt decidedly unscientific, because how do you know if the mallards you've just counted are coming or going? I was pondering joining the Toronto Ornithological Club, and at that time they still asked to see a birding CV. I thought that participating in a CBC would bolster my credentials.

There was, of course, the anxiety of venturing out into the birding world alone for the first time, without the comfort of my Saturday bird group, and without Brete's eyes and ears to act as my guide. And there was the slight matter of explaining my skill level.

"I'd love to participate in a Christmas Bird Count, but I'm a beginner birder. However, what I lack in knowledge, I make up for in enthusiasm," I e-mailed. I wasn't exaggerating. I had only been birding for a couple of years—my binocular skills were lacking, my birding by ear non-existent. Thankfully, winter birding requires substantially less song recognition than spring birding does, since most birds don't sing outside of breeding season. The adaptability of birds far exceeds what I had imagined: when not in active breeding mode, the reproductive organs that send signals to an avian songbird's voice box actually shrink to a fraction of their size. To assuage the potential red flag that my skill level posed to any team in question, I mentioned the blog post that I'd been hired to write for ON Nature about my first CBC experience.

Whoever read my e-mail put me in touch with a gentleman named Don Barnett who, within a matter of hours, invited me to join his team in Earl Bales Park, no questions asked. I woke up to rain on the day of the CBC, which didn't bode well for eight hours spent outside counting birds, and then made the grave error of wearing Icelandic woollens for the occasion. By about ten o'clock, I smelled like a sheep and the odour didn't dissipate for the entire day. But camaraderie at these events is a top priority and nobody said a word.

We were a motley crew. Apart from Don, who was in his eighties and one of the most hardy individuals I'd ever met, there was Leslie, who proudly called herself the Bird Lady of North York; Anne-Marie, the president-elect of the Toronto Ornithological Club; a friend of hers who did frequent reptile counts for the Toronto Zoo; and Howard, who, in addition to being an avid birder and helping Don with the hawk watch in High Park, was also a doctor and a public health official for the city of Toronto.

"You mean to tell me that there are *doctors* who watch birds?" my grandmother said the next day. "Is he Jewish?"

"I think so."

"Now that's something." My grandmother had no interest in hearing about how Don, who was two years her senior, could climb hills and withstand the elements, or that the president of Toronto's biggest birding club was a woman, but she couldn't stop asking questions about Howard. Not only did my acquaintance with Howard somehow elevate me in the hierarchy of Toronto social capital, but it also presented a conundrum for my grandmother. Here was a birder she could not make fun of. But she couldn't resist adding, "Doesn't he have anything better to do?"

"I think for some people it's a passion."

"Going out in the rain for eight hours and counting birds is a passion? I hope you didn't sit on anything cold out there." Any time spent outside posed an imminent threat to my reproductive organs, which, though my grandmother didn't dare say it, needed all the coddling they could get.

Winter is hardly the most exciting time of year for birding in Toronto, and winter birding far from the lake is even less exciting. Our quadrant didn't boast large numbers of waterfowl, and the potential for owls was minimal. The most we could hope for were winter finches, which I had never heard of. But I was a beginner, and everything felt exciting to me. A downy woodpecker pounding his heart out took me by surprise. Every American robin I saw still had the allure of mystery. As I raised my binoculars I wondered, what if this is the rarity? Though I'd only been birding for a couple of years, I secretly hoped to see something truly noteworthy and impress the group with my unintentional *savoir faire*; I accepted my beginner status, but I started to want more.

At one point Howard heard some chip notes, uttered a single word, "crossbills," and bolted up a muddy hill. I had no idea what he meant and why it mattered, nor why nobody was shocked to see him slide down sideways, as if on a snowboard, while the muddy ground collided with his thighs. A crossbill sighting was clearly worth the near-death experience.

"I definitely heard the white-winged crossbill, and I think I caught a glimpse of it, but I'm not completely sure. Did anyone else hear that rapid series of notes?"

Don nodded in agreement and I stood there wondering what it was they had heard, apart from the raindrops pounding down on our heads.

Just as Howard began to clean the mud off his rain pants, Leslie shouted, "Fourteen mallards overhead" and Anne-Marie caught sight of a flock of seven goldfinches. Every time I tried to contribute a sighting, it turned out to be an American robin.

"Do you hear that nasal sound?" Don asked.

"I think so." That was my truthful answer. I wasn't sure I knew what he was talking about, but I'd heard something and it might as well have been nasal.

"That's a white-breasted nuthatch. We should get both species today."

"The one that looks like a chickadee?"

"Well, not really. Their shape is different, and the nuthatch likes to creep down tree trunks. Chickadees never do that." I'd struggled with these two species for a while, but Don's description finally helped me distinguish them: nuthatches crept down a tree headfirst, neck straining forward and elevated slightly, just as I aspired to do in yoga class when striking a Cobra pose. I wondered whether the bird was uncomfortable, but I didn't have the time to ponder further because I heard a sound from up above and pointed my binoculars upward, wanting desperately to be in two places at once.

"What's that sound? Is that another nuthatch?"

"No, that's a cardinal. It's missing the nasal tone." Right. Of course it was. "Wait, and there's the female. Make that four cardinals total."

Somebody registered excitement at the sight of a hairy woodpecker, but I still lacked the skill to distinguish it from a downy and let the pedagogical moment go.

"Overhead, nine Canada geese."

"I think I see a red-tail up in that tree." We all looked and, indeed, there was a hawk resting calmly on a branch toward the top, but by that point I had little interest. I was wet and could think of little else apart from lunch. My curiosity was fading fast and my patience even faster.

Nobody else seemed to share my frustration. Everybody brought their own bagged lunch and we sat in a deserted and overheated Parks and Recreation pavilion catching our breath, refuelling and getting our list in order. Whoever scribed that day had missed a few key items, and we made sure to fill in the blanks.

"I'm positive I heard a pileated woodpecker," Anne-Marie said.

"Put it on the list."

I had heard of a pileated woodpecker but had not yet seen one and had no idea what it sounded like. All I knew was that it drummed oversized oval-shaped holes in trees.

"Are you really going to write about us?"

"Of course."

"Only nice things!"

"We'd better behave. She's a writer."

I wondered, for a minute, what it meant to misbehave on a Christmas Bird Count. Shout out the wrong number of Canada geese?

"How do you know you're not counting the same bird twice?" I asked.

"It's hard when they fly back and forth. We make educated guesses. We just try our best." Citizen science isn't exactly scientific, I wanted to say—but didn't.

After lunch, still soaking wet, I did my best to participate. I started counting, without understanding exactly what the point was, and realized that understanding wasn't the most important part. I focused on the robins, cardinals, goldfinches and Canada geese, the four species I could safely ID. I let someone else take care of the sparrows, which all looked the same to me.

"Otherwise known as LBJ."

"What?"

"Little Brown Job. The nickname for sparrows that are tricky to ID."

I wanted to tell them that at this point nearly every species felt like an LBJ to me. Even the colourful ones never looked like the colour the field guide promised. I learned that the green-grey-brown palette is often subjective, as is the word *rufous*, which often only hinted at the notion of red, so subtle I nearly always missed it, and *buffy*, which could mean anything from buttery yellow to off-white. Blue and purple also differed for nearly every observer.

The more I counted, the more closely I paid attention. Everyone on my count had at least five CBCs under their belt, and Don probably had forty or fifty. Most of them recognized bird population patterns, frequently noting how many more goldfinches they had counted the previous year or waxing nostalgic about the year they had an eastern screech owl on the count.

Birders are fanatical about counting. Birds seen, kilometres driven, birds not seen, birds *promised* to be seen, birds *hoped* to be seen. Checklists are taken very seriously. But it's not just an obsessive activity; counting is a way of tracking time – and variation over time. It's a way of making sense of our surroundings. I don't remember ever learning how to count as a child. It happened imperceptibly. But here I felt like I was relearning the mechanism for the first time.

I don't remember our exact tally for the day, but it must have been modest. We tried to supplement it with a trip to a nearby cemetery and a science school located in a ravine. We added a few waterfowl to the species count. Feet frozen, I abandoned the group at three o'clock and headed home, deciding to skip the party, which included a final tally of birds from all twenty-one Toronto quadrants. I didn't think I could handle hearing a rundown of every single bird species, and by this point I felt intimidated by everybody's knowledge.

On that first Christmas Bird Count, I hoped for miracles. I had wanted to be the precocious beginner who unexpectedly found a rarity, the underdog team member whose performance stunned everybody. In the end, I wrote my blog post, sent it to the group leader and never heard from any of them again. I took a two-year hiatus from CBCs.

The Glamour of Birding

WHEN I CONTEMPLATED BIRDING AS A HOBBY, I THOUGHT IT would be a great way to spend time in beautiful places. I saw photos of people on the Platte River in Nebraska looking for whooping cranes. I was spellbound by images of people birding among the gargantuan saguaro cacti in southern Arizona, marvelling at desert birds, and others looking for California condors in Grand Canyon National Park. I imagined the thrill of seeing the endemic birds of Hawaii while visiting volcanoes and mile-long white sand beaches. Birds would take me to the most exotic locales, I reasoned.

But the glamour of birds is of a different nature. Birds don't hang out in stunning, manicured locations. Of course, there is the exotic travel, but the more ordinary, down-home birding where one practises one's shorebird and waterfowl identification skills occurs in places where non-birders wouldn't tread of their own volition. Birds are partial to dumpsters—and especially to industrial areas with feral grasses growing uncontrollably.

BY THE TIME I RETURNED TO THE CHRISTMAS BIRD COUNT, two years after my first experience, birding for eight hours in the rain while constantly misidentifying robins, I knew a few more people in the birding community. When my friend Justin invited me to join his sector, I looked it up on a map and accepted the offer immediately. Sector 16B looked like it belonged to Tommy Thompson Park, my favourite pocket of city wilderness, and I imagined us walking along the peninsula's coastline in search of snowy owls on the rocks, traipsing through shrubs to look for northern saw-whet owls, catching sight of a northern shrike on the way to the lighthouse at the tip. It turned out that I'd misread the map and confused my sector with its neighbour, the storied sector 16A. Instead of walking to the lighthouse, I'd agreed to bird the northern edge of the park and an area called the Port Lands, an industrial eyesore left over from the days when the city had tried to build up its reputation as a serious port.

Justin designated me as the scribe, a role I didn't initially want on account of the cold. It's not too hard to keep a running count of every bird seen, but it's a challenge to accomplish the task in minus-ten-degree weather, when my hands would rather be in my pockets. But more surprising was that as I was scribing and counting, I paid greater attention. I had previously let others do the work for me. Part of the beauty of counting involves acknowledging the world around us. Suddenly, I sensed the importance of my role. I was documenting all the bird life within the boundaries of my specific sector, which we criss-crossed by foot and by car.

We spent over an hour counting birds in Toronto's recycling yard.

"Why are we here?" I couldn't help asking. Given how much trash is thrown out along with recycled materials, the place had a more potent odour than one might have liked.

"Wait until you see the domestic pigeon condominium," Justin said. As a CBC leader, Justin is ideal; he takes his duties extremely seriously and doesn't miss a square metre of our quadrant. Indeed, we came upon an abandoned trailer that someone had converted into a glorious abode for white domestic pigeons, complete with tiered balconies and more food than the birds knew what to do with.

"I'd live there," I said. I wouldn't, but Justin's earnest desire to show off the pigeon digs seemed to warrant some kind of affirmation.

We counted large numbers of gulls, and just when I started to doze off in the car, Danny yelled, "Kestrel!"

My favourite raptor by far. I jumped out of the car, pulled my binoculars up and marvelled at the bird's fantastic colour scheme. Whoever designed the American kestrel's plumage must have been an artist who knew that a brightly rust-coloured back set off by denim wings would work to awesome effect.

Danny Miles turned out to be the other surprise of our CBC team. When I arrived to meet the group, I noticed that one of us didn't really look like the rest. Long hair parted in the middle, with a scruffy beard, Danny Miles was a rock star. I had never birded with a rock star before. Actually, I'm not sure I'd ever even met a rock star.

"Would I have heard of your band?" I asked.

"Depends what kind of music you like."

"Mostly classical. I listen to a lot of Mahler and Bach."

"Nope. You definitely wouldn't have heard of my band."

"Well, I'll look you up on YouTube."

"Uh...it might not exactly be your thing. But who knows? Anyhow, we're called July Talk." I later learned that Danny Miles was the drummer for a Juno-winning band.

And from there we moved straight to birds, which Danny had discovered when on tour in Australia a few years before. Since then, he's been taking photos of birds everywhere he goes, and he started a website called Drummers Who Love Birds (drummerswholovebirds.com). Apparently, he's not alone.

Our celebrity bird that year was the harlequin duck.

"You might get histrionic when you see this duck for the first time," Justin said to Danny on our way to the Unwin Street bridge, where the duck had last been seen.

"Why is that?"

"Because the Latin binomial for the Harlequin is *Histrionicus histrionicus*." I explained Justin's bird joke, and Danny stood there staring.

"You guys are hilarious."

And then we caught sight of the regal visitor as he glistened in the mid-morning winter light, his white facial markings glowing. We stood there, star-struck, entirely oblivious to the electrical generating station smokestacks in the background. The slate-blue body and chestnut-brown sides were set off by white stripes around the neck and along the back, as if someone had hand-painted this marvel. He stood out among the dozens of greater scaups, redheads, long-tails and buffleheads; he glided among them nonchalantly, head high, confident that all those people with binoculars standing on the shore had their eyes fixed on him alone.

But our CBC pièce de résistance that day was the Ashbridges Bay Water Treatment Plant, which we managed to enter because our rival team in the next quadrant had connections and knew somebody who knew somebody. In we went to count waterfowl. Not only were we birding in an area that most Toronto residents have never heard of, but we were birding in a labyrinthine structure with dozens of pools of varying chemical composition and temperature, all designed to filter and clean out human waste. If someone had shown me aerial photos of the place, I might have confused it with an Eastern European spa that boasts a vast array of swimming pools, some of which smell so strongly of sulphur that it both clears the sinuses and makes you gag instantly.

Justin's strategic decision to team up with our rivals in 16A raised our numbers by 814 mallards, 542 gadwalls, a few northern shovelers and a lone, seductive-looking northern pintail. Unremarkable vistas aside, our sector proved productive, both in terms of species diversity and numbers. So productive that we won the CBC "Hole Truth" Award, which amounts to a trophy in the shape of a tree trunk with a hole in it—a distinction perhaps best not bragged about. A group photo of us ended up on one of Toronto's top birder websites and there we are, all eight of us, shivering in the minus-ten-degree temperature, smiling with pride for having earned our badge of honour navigating terrain that comes as close as one can get to a city's underworld.

SMELLY SEWAGE LAGOONS ARE ANOTHER FAVOURITE PLACE to watch birds. A report of a red-necked phalarope once brought Brete and me to Port Perry's sewage lagoon. We parked at the town dump and spent twenty minutes roaming the dispossessed refrigerators and sundry electronics before meeting with a civil servant who had me sign a release form—in exchange for twenty dollars, he presented me with a four-digit code that promised to give me access to the water treatment facility and the secret world of phalaropes. The home appliance graveyard had an eerie feel to it; how many of these air conditioners and refrigerators had outlived their owners or been replaced on account of a breakup? How many had simply died a natural death? I saw a fridge that resembled my family's old fridge with the freezer at eye level, always over-stocked. Here stood its twin sibling, doors open, innards showing—a pathetic, disembodied spectacle. Without photos, artwork and magnets decorating the front door, its blank gaze startled me.

When we arrived at the water treatment facility, it turned out that the lock was open and we entered without even punching in my twenty-dollar code. Birders look out for one another. That day, I saw my first red-necked phalarope dancing giddily in the water and learned the term *reverse sexual dimorphism*—female phalaropes are among the few birds that are more brightly coloured than their male counterparts. It would have been even more thrilling had we seen the female in breeding plumage, but the Port Perry sewage lagoon in southern Ontario isn't exactly the Arctic.

There is nothing appetizing about sewage lagoons, but birds are besotted with the microorganisms in the sewage, as well as the insects that hang out amidst our waste. Nobody would choose to go there—unless they're a birder—and most people don't even know they exist unless they work in plumbing or urban planning or happen to live along a country road next to a plant and occasionally get a whiff of something foul. We birders stand in the midst of it and marvel at the strangeness of it all—at the fact that somehow this has become our life, that we derive pleasure from it in earnest, and that we're penetrating a secret pocket that nobody else has access to. As a birder, my parameters of looking have changed; what used to be unsavoury has now been transformed into a specialized habitat, something piquant, a thing of unlikely beauty. I see things I wouldn't have thought to look at before.

The day I saw my first phalarope, I observed myself from a distance. Who was that person standing there, one foot firmly planted in goose shit, inhaling the scent of decomposing raw waste water, with binoculars glued to her eyes, a Tilley hat—with the string contraption that she now wears under her chin when it's windy—fixed to her head, furiously trying to determine whether she's looking at a solitary sandpiper or a white-rumped sandpiper? How had she become this person who knows that an osprey nests on the telephone pole directly south of the water treatment plant? The person who woke up at 5:00 a.m. to stand within arm's length of human waste to find birds?

Hope

WHEN I SAW MY FIRST KITTIWAKE, I WAS BARELY INTER-
ested in the fact that it was a kittiwake. I was in Iceland,
hiking between Arnarstapi and Hellnar on the Snæfellsnes
peninsula, and the inside of the cliff was dotted with
kittiwakes.

"What are these seagulls?" Leon asked. I didn't know
which problem to tackle first. Leon had just uttered the
word *seagull*, which violates a cardinal law of birding,
since seagulls don't actually exist as a species. I know from
experience the extent to which seagulls send birders into
orbit. The first time I used the word, Brete was quick to
inform me, after an exasperated sigh and some intense
head-shaking, that the word was a colloquialism for gulls,
of which there are approximately 150 species worldwide.
The problem even more pressing than the lexical issue was
that the birds I was looking at left me cold.

"Definitely kittiwakes and other things I can't ID."

"Kittiwakes? But you've wanted to see a kittiwake for
years. Why aren't you screaming and going crazy the way
you usually do?" Leon referred to my unbridled response

to seeing my first red-headed woodpecker, which I'd told him about.

"I've been seeing them every day since we've been here."

"And you don't care anymore?"

The rarity of a bird depends on where you are, geographically. When I saw my first tricoloured heron, the bird's physique, coupled with the unreal feeling that I'd found it on my own, forced me straight to the ground, where I had to catch my breath. But later that winter I travelled to Curaçao, where tricoloured herons come close to being backyard birds. But I think it also depends on whether the bird you're after is a nemesis bird—the one you dream of seeing but that eludes you at every turn. If it were a scissor-tailed flycatcher, which I've now missed in Toronto three times, I'd probably be in raptures.

But all this for a gull? I don't mean to disparage larophiles. On the contrary, I wish I loved gulls with such fervour that I had the patience, curiosity and radical attention to detail to distinguish first- from second-year plumage. I envied Justin's intense commitment to understanding gulls, even though I laughed at him on our Christmas Bird Count, when he insisted on filming and narrating the surprise appearance of an Iceland gull sitting atop a pile of rubble in the company of a hundred or so herring gulls. That he could liken the squeaky vocalizations of a herring gull flying overhead to a lullaby is, in and of itself, a thing of wonder.

MY FIRST ATTEMPT TO FIND A KITTIWAKE WAS IN NIAGARA Falls, a few years earlier, in December, when the Niagara area becomes a gull bonanza. Hundreds of birders descend on the area, looking for gull rarities. Ontario Field

Ornithologists commemorate the spectacle by organizing the Gull Celebration Weekend, replete with an identification workshop and quiz. Loving gulls is a test in hardiness because the conditions are almost always awful. Harassed by a combination of wind, rain or snow, larophiles will watch these birds for hours. Being among them has given me the chance to survey birding apparel and finally convinced me to adopt rain pants as a sartorial staple. The rewards for hours at the mercy of the elements are significant—for those who know how to interpret them.

Although I had been birding for over five years, every encounter with gulls still humbled me and brought me right back to my beginner days. Gulls present a unique challenge, not only because most of them look similar, but also because plumage varies drastically depending on the age of a bird. To think that a juvenile and adult herring gull are related is to suspend disbelief in earnest.

Watching gulls requires a different level of patience from looking up at warblers. Differentiating between warblers—even in fall plumage—is challenging, but possible. Watching gulls really does feel like staring at a *Where's Waldo?* book, only instead of the red-and-white-striped sweater, this version of Waldo is dressed just one shade removed from the thousands of other gulls just like him.

When we got to the Niagara Whirlpool, we looked down and I saw approximately three thousand gulls of various persuasions circling below. Someone kept shouting "Kittiwake!" and others followed with their binoculars. For about twenty minutes, I too followed a gull, which I later learned to be a Bonaparte. The longer I looked, the more it grew before my eyes, until I realized that I was in a trance and had been looking at not one but possibly a dozen different birds. By that point, my fingers had frozen and it was time for lunch.

The botched kittiwake sighting meant that we had time to look for the razorbill in Niagara-on-the-Lake.

Had it not been for the kittiwake, I wouldn't have seen the razorbill.

I knew it was a rare bird for southern Ontario, but I didn't realize just how rare. I hadn't done my research that morning—or any morning during the first five years I birded—not just on account of laziness, but because I was still afraid to commit to this hobby-cum-lifestyle. The razorbill is a pelagic bird, typically nesting in sea cliffs, which aren't exactly prominent in southern Ontario. It's also the closest living relative to the extinct great auk, which would have meant nothing to me at the time, but now makes me feel that I'd been in the presence of something majestic and perilously close to extinction, in a secret communion with history.

After searching furiously for the kittiwake in the dizzying Whirlpool, here the razorbill was the only largish bird in sight. I didn't have to search hard because it appeared in my binoculars' view and there was no head bobbing or frantically waving about. It was just there and I wondered if someone had hand-drawn the white line on its face.

I THINK OF THAT DAY OFTEN. THE DISASTERS AND THE MIS-takes are often just that—a road to something other, something different, something arguably better. I think of my first marriage sometimes. The ways in which I failed my ex-husband; the ways in which, toward the end, we were awful to one another. I tried to retrace my steps many a time, tried apologizing, tried rekindling, but it was too late. Things were over. Years later, I realized that, had I not had that disastrous first marriage—the relationship that showed me the capacity I had to ruin something and to hurt someone out of my own self-preservation—I never would have met Leon.

Niagara-on-the-Lake used to register in my mind as the place where we saw summer theatre, but now it's home to my razorbill sighting in 2011. The bird I didn't know was extraordinary. The bird I wouldn't have seen had the kittiwake worked out. We talk about destiny, about what's meant to be, when in reality it's usually a combination of failure plus time, a series of adjusted circumstances, a question of human resilience and ability to reconfigure our expectations.

What I love about birding isn't so much the birds I see but the circumstances within which I see them. That seeing the birds allows me to reflect on my own life, to forgive myself for things I've done, or to understand how they might not have happened otherwise.

There have been so many botched kittiwake sightings in my life. It's hard not to see them as colossal mistakes. It's hard to know when to call them off, when to back off and try for something new.

The day we saw the razorbill, we had no assurance that it would be there. But we hoped.

Life Lessons

SOMETHING HAPPENS WHEN I WALK INTO A HAIR SALON. I lose the ability to formulate coherent thoughts. Once, when I was fifteen, unable to tell my hairdresser what I wanted, I let my mother speak for me: her vision included raspy bangs and a layered haircut that, once executed, sent me into hysterical sobs. Maybe it doesn't help that every time I sit down in my hairdresser's chair, I think of my aunt Dora, who arrived on Staten Island in the late 1970s, from Kiev, and worked in a small hair salon with her sister, Inna. In her broken English, she once asked a client if he wanted his haircut accompanied by a blow job. In her émigré lexicon, the words "blow job" and "blow dry" were one and the same.

I've had a lifelong struggle with my hair. I don't fault my actual hair follicles, because they're enviable, producing hair that is abundant, strong and fast growing, with relatively little grey for my age. My hair has never done exactly what I want it to do, but the problem lies deeper than that. My entire life, I've had a vision of an Ur-Hairdo, a hairdo to end all hairdos, one that will become my signature hairdo and will elevate me beyond the domain of hair woes. Sometimes before I see Randy, my hairdresser, I anxiously leaf through magazines, searching for the hair arrangement that most closely resembles my ideal. Eventually I give up because all the coiffures look far too labour-intensive, and also because I can't really tell which one will properly grace my features. I acknowledge my usual mess of contradictions: once I told Randy that I wanted the feel of a look with bangs without actually having bangs, and the effect of layers while maintaining a straight line.

I have a photo of me as a three-year-old clad in a gingham shirt, talking on a rotary-dial phone. I used to spend hours talking to myself. In that photo, I'm sporting a thick bob, with a hint of bangs that fall to the side naturally. In reality what held them in place so perfectly was probably sweat, because my parents dressed me in Soviet-bloc woollens from head to toe no matter the weather, and even after we emigrated the Yugoslavian long underwear followed along, as did the prickly Bulgarian socks and the Czechoslovakian sweaters. My childhood memories are all accompanied by a fear of catching a cold by inadvertently sitting in the way of a draft. The best way to prevent that from happening, we believed, was to keep oneself swaddled in woollens; in all my early photos, I'm sweating. And yet that's the photo I think back to every time, the photo that I try to describe to Randy, the way my hair hung effortlessly, the way the back maintained its shape with nary a blow dryer involved.

I FIRST SAW A CEDAR WAXWING, *BOMBYCILLA CEDRORUM*, IN Luther Marsh, a few hours north of Toronto. It has a black eye mask—almost as if it's wearing a fetching pair of

Ray-Bans—and a slick, cinnamon, gravity-defying crest on its head. Its style is not as ostentatious as a northern cardinal's, which basically screams, "Look at me! Look at me NOW," but it's still full of grace, and even something beyond grace. It wasn't one cedar waxwing that we saw but a flock that alighted on different branches of the same tree, and I was immediately struck by the birds' effortless yet perfect hairdos. This is a bird that never has to stand in front of the mirror wondering whether mousse or gel or some sort of pomade will do the trick and finally abandoning all three overpriced options in favour of a ponytail or, better yet, a hair clip. This is a bird without hair issues. This is a bird I'd love to be.

A number of years later, when I started volunteering at a bird banding station and began my treacherous journey toward learning how to extract birds from the lightweight mist nets, I held a cedar waxwing in my hand. Not only that, but I managed to extract the bird from the net, which turned out to be easier than I had assumed, since it wasn't tangled and simply slid out. Nervously, I held the waxwing in bander's grip, with the head snug between my index and middle fingers, and the rest of the bird's body in my cupped hand. I could feel the bird's heartbeat knocking against my shaking hand.

I knew waxwings had silky plumage—hence their genus *Bombycilla,* which derives from the Latin for silkworm—but I gasped at the softness of the bird's feathers. It wasn't just that they were soft, they were miraculously soft, something almost otherworldly, like sensing an unexpected kinship, reaching toward a hand that suddenly felt familiar.

Just as I inspected the bird's hairdo up close and marvelled at my superhuman feat of actually handling the bird, holding it in my hands without killing it, the cedar waxwing spat up three plump red berries, one of which, semi-masticated, stained my khakis. So much for the resplendent beauty of nature. There is absolutely nothing cute, passive or demure about birds, soft, silky plumage notwithstanding.

I stared at the cedar waxwings in Luther Marsh and wondered what it must be like to go through life knowing that your hair will be the envy of everybody. But when I encountered my first Ross's goose, I experienced something even better: the beauty of not caring.

Had I known what to expect, I would have cancelled all my afternoon plans and driven straight to the Royal Botanical Gardens in Burlington. I would not have waited, because to see a Ross's goose is to witness first-hand the concept of pure, unadulterated confidence. But the stop for the Ross's goose was unexpected: on our way back from looking for a Wilson's snipe that decided not to materialize, near Hamilton, Heather quickly read a report on ONTBIRDS, informing us that the Ross's goose in Burlington had not yet absconded.

By that point I was feeling the disappointment of a snipeless day acutely. It was mid-March, and I'd had my fill of snowy owl sightings. I was eager to announce that spring had begun. A snipe sighting would have been the perfect harbinger. Instead, we sifted through reeds and grasses and left empty-handed. Snipe disappointment aside, I'd also never thought of myself as a Goose Gal. It's hard for me to take geese seriously because they're ubiquitous; I see them every day in the parking lot, in parks, flying over the lake. (It's hard to believe that there was once a time when Canada geese were an endangered species in Toronto.) The thought of mustering excitement over a potential goose sighting was tiring. Even the fact that it would be a bird I could add to my life list left me unimpressed.

When we arrived at the Royal Botanical Gardens parking lot, we immediately noticed congregations of Canada geese. They milled about in large flocks, perhaps discussing the weather or contemplating the strange-looking creature in their midst. All uniformly brown-bodied, with long black necks and white cheeks, these geese were the only other birds apart from pigeons that I had been familiar with prior to my red-winged blackbird sighting. So ubiquitous were they in my urban landscape that I think I failed to think of them as birds.

And here, at home in the company of these giants, roamed a lone white, diminutive Ross's goose. Described by Sibley as a "miniature Snow Goose," the words fail to do the goose's strangeness justice. Miniature indeed, but with all its proportions slightly off; the bill seems smaller than it ought to be for the size of the neck, and the body bulkier than the head size would warrant.

And yet, infelicity of proportion aside, the Ross's goose parades with such confidence you'd think he were Napoleon. At first, I felt a little pity for the poor Ross's goose—I would have felt out of my league amidst birds that dwarfed me—but he didn't seem to mind. On the contrary, he stood upright and ambled elegantly, occasionally grazing on the hillside, never exhibiting a moment of self-doubt. I marvelled at this sight: not only was his stature miniature compared with the others, not only did he look slightly ridiculous, but he was so busy ambling proudly, so entirely delighted with his station in life, that he didn't once stop to compare himself with the giants around him.

I found myself coveting the confidence of a Ross's goose. And suddenly, just like that, I had transformed into a Goose Gal. When I closed my eyes, I could see the dainty bill of the Ross's goose, and could imagine him parading majestically, head high. I thought of his posture when I attempted a *retiré* in *relevé* in my ballet class and couldn't hold my balance properly. I thought of him as I ventured into a lopsided pirouette—though I could see in the mirror that nothing looked quite as it ought to, I thought back to little-man Ross, who strutted his stuff without the least concern for how he might appear to others. Following his lead, I challenged myself to smile at my reflection.

Ross's goose is named in honour of Bernard Rogan Ross, who in the nineteenth century was a chief trader with the Hudson's Bay Company and while at Fort Simpson in the Northwest Territories was in charge of the Mackenzie River District. A natural history aficionado, Ross eventually submitted over 2,200 specimens to the Smithsonian Institution. In honour of his contribution to ornithology, Spencer Fullerton Braid, assistant secretary of the Smithsonian Institution, named the goose after him.

Where did Ross house his 2,200 specimens, I wondered, and how many geese did he shoot before he recognized it as a species distinct from the snow goose? But mostly I wondered about him up north in the frigid Northwest Territories and whether he was ever homesick. The first time I saw a northern landscape was in Iceland, in 2000. My then-husband had been teaching a philosophy seminar at a university there, and I joined him for a long weekend, not knowing exactly where I was going. Once I arrived and saw the crystalline light and the variations of greying sky, I couldn't look away. It was early November and the days were damp and darkening, yet light filtered through at unpredictable intervals, fleetingly, but engulfing everything. I knew what it meant to fall in love with the north, a primal place that made me reassess my understanding of the word *landscape*. That light—Ross must have shared it too. But how did he survive those long, dark months of winter? Maybe that's when he prepared his specimens.

I wonder about those accidental ornithologists who seem to have fallen in love with birds in much the same way I did. What did Bernard Ross see that got him hooked? Perhaps he took note of the confident strut of the bird that was to become his namesake and it all tumbled from there.

That day in Burlington, I stood there watching a Ross's goose manoeuvre his way through the crowds of Canada geese, pausing every so often to peck at something on the ground. I watched him saunter about without a care in the world and I wondered about every decision I had made to get here, to this place, watching this goose promenade with glee.

Ross's goose turned out to be the tip of the goose iceberg. Two years later, I was the one driving two hours in search of a riotous goose party: I joined a bird group that had learned that Lee Brown Marsh—a pond in the vicinity of Long Point Provincial Park which anybody in their right mind would overlook unless they were on a goose chase of sorts—had a four-species goose bonanza: snow, cackling, greater white-fronted and Canada. The pond is a square little thing in the middle of flat agricultural land, not exactly a natural wonder. And yet that day, it transformed into just that.

We found the snow goose fairly quickly, since it looks like a more robust version of a Ross's goose but, as the field guides assert, slightly less "cute." The greater white-fronted goose requires a suspension of disbelief. To think that nature—or evolution—would create a bird of this ilk: a creature closely resembling a Canada goose, but with a white circle around its pink bill, as if the goose had dipped the front of his face in whipped cream. To top off the peculiarities, the bird sports bright orange legs. But unlike Ross's geese, greater white-fronted geese move about in flocks, huddling close to one another, perhaps demanding emotional support to mitigate the impact of their curious appearance.

(I must admit that my fascination with geese ended at the sight of a cackling goose, which I could only differentiate from a Canada goose by virtue of its size, and even then only with a trained professional by my side pointing out the discrepancies in length and overall proportions.)

I NO LONGER CRY AFTER MY HAIRCUTS, BUT THERE'S ALWAYS a moment of shock when I look at myself in the mirror and can't quite register the difference between feverish hope (that I might resemble a cedar waxwing) and result (that I am still me). It isn't scientifically right to anthropomorphize, to see yourself in a bird, connecting with birds as if they were humans, and yet that's how I fell in love with birds, and started to see them as part of my own landscape. Because after a few years of looking through binoculars, I started seeing them everywhere, and if asked who I'd most want to resemble, I'd have to say it in bird-speak: I'd like a cedar waxwing's hair, a northern flicker's intrepid sense of style, a Ross's goose's superlative confidence, the mellifluous singing voice of a wood thrush, a belted kingfisher's singular glare, a winter wren's capacity to be heard, a northern gannet's fierce single-minded determination, a black-and-white warbler's awesome, classic elegance, and a red-winged blackbird's ability to make a first impression.

Nemesis Birds

I AVERAGE QUARTERLY VISITS TO SEWAGE LAGOONS AND decided to return to Port Perry with my friends Martha and Monika because of a reported shorebird extravaganza.

A children's librarian with a particular fondness for alliteration, Martha charmed me the day she admitted that her desire to visit Algonquin Park in the winter stemmed from her insatiable "fever for finches." But with shore-birds, it's different: Martha has the preternatural patience required to puzzle through identifying them and comb through every square inch of water surface in order to find the lone lurker. What Martha feels for shorebirds is more like an affinity or an identification; it goes beyond love. Sometimes she looks at them so intently that I get the feel-ing she wants to *be* a shorebird. Her former colleague and current BBF (Best Birding Friend), Monika, claims to love them too, but I sometimes see her eyes wander. Monika is a self-proclaimed craniac and can't get enough of sandhill cranes. Like me, after a few hours of shorebird observation, Monika is ready for a snack in town, but, left to her own devices, Martha would keep looking. When her husband accompanies her on these shorebird expeditions, he brings a book and a lawn chair.

On this particular day, we didn't have to stop at the town dump because Martha had filled out the paperwork and paid the fee online, in preparation for our expedition. Instead, we bolted straight for the shorebirds, giggled as we passed the sign for Cobbledick Road on the 401, and arrived in just under two hours. After three hours spent dutifully scanning each of the sewage ponds, we still couldn't tear Martha away from the shorebirds: she meticulously gathered all the requisite field marks, one by one, until she managed to identify a mystery bird as a stilt sandpiper with reasonable authority. I failed to detect what Sibley called its "long drooping bill," which seemed identical to the slightly shorter, straighter bill of the greater yellowlegs, no matter how hard I looked. While Martha kept deliberating, Monika and I bonded over our shared nemesis bird, the pileated woodpecker. We'd both heard them and I'd seen one in flight, but I craved a full-frontal view. The largest woodpecker and the one that most closely resembles the extinct ivory-billed woodpecker, the pileated had eluded me for over five years. We proceeded to trade pileated non-sightings, trying to outdo one another and determine who held the most spectacular failed sighting. In birding, failures count almost as much as successes.

Just as I regaled her with my last attempt, which resulted in seeing at least twenty enormous, oval-shaped, pileated-drilled tree holes and hearing the clear pounding, Monika whispered, "Oh my god, it's him!"

"What are you talking about?"

And she pointed skyward, to where a pileated wood-pecker flew in slow motion over our heads, landed in the tree directly in our line of vision, and posed. Monika stood there shaking, her finger still pointing at the bird. She stood there in shock for so long that she almost forgot to take a photo. Once she put her camera down, I saw that her eyes were red.

Monika was crying out of shock and joy and at the serendipity of the sighting. We'd both been birding long enough to know that moments like this need to be celebrated.

But I held back tears because I felt loss almost as clearly as happiness. There's only ever one first sighting, and now I'd never be able to long for a pileated woodpecker sighting in the same way. I wanted to commit every second of the experience to memory, but I couldn't: the bird had appeared when we least expected it—and disappeared as soon as Monika had snapped a series of photos. In a sense it was pure luck, but in another we made it happen by doing what we had to do as birders: we showed up, we paid attention to the world around us, we scanned, we listened, we hoped, we imagined, we waited. For every ten target birds that elude you, there's one that makes a surprise appearance, and that moment is celestial.

Martha tried to share in our pileated woodpecker enthusiasm, but I could see that she still inhabited her stilt sandpiper reverie. We walked a bit farther, and Monika and I kept glancing back to the tree where we still imagined we saw the flaming red crest of the pileated as he tilted his head back precariously, even though he'd long since flown away.

But now that my nemesis bird was no longer my nemesis, what next? The sense of loss lingered as we drove back to the city. Of course there were hundreds of tropical birds that I wanted to see—motmots, frigatebirds, boobies and bowerbirds whose exotic colours, names, shapes and bizarre behaviours I hoped to lay eyes on—but their distance from my world was so great that I never properly longed for them.

Nor had I ever chased them and failed. There's something about the unfulfilled desire inspired by a nemesis bird that keeps one coming back for more. Whereas the pleasure of seeing a target bird can be intense and overwhelming, the pain of not seeing a desired bird is even more memorable. Tolstoy said it best in the first line of *Anna Karenina*: "All happy families are alike, but each unhappy family is unhappy in its own way." Emotional anguish is always more interesting than pleasure, and the pursuit of a nemesis bird feels more singular than actually seeing it.

Not having a nemesis bird is the saddest thing in the world.

And then I remembered the Bohemian waxwing. Three years into birding with Brete's group, I went on a winter outing that took us two hours northeast of Toronto, to an area usually visited in the spring, when wildflowers carpet the Carden Alvar plain. The barren, snow-covered landscape on an overcast day didn't inspire confidence and gave me extra reason to start counting down the days to spring. Lucy was in the midst of a vigorous chemotherapy and radiation regimen but had the strength to join us that day. When I heard her gasp at the mention of Bohemian waxwings in the car, I looked them up in Sibley. To me they just seemed like a greyer, larger, fatter version of a cedar waxwing, but I kept my disappointment to myself.

"The Bohemians were seen on Monck Road just yesterday," Brete said. "I think it's worth a try. We're just twenty minutes away."

In Brete's lexicon, twenty minutes meant the whole enterprise would take at least an hour.

We got them within five minutes of arriving at Monck Road. Foraging in a juniper tree, mixed in with a flock of cedar waxwings, they were exactly as underwhelming as they had seemed to me in the field guide. I couldn't distinguish their rusty undertail feathers or the sharp white rectangle marks on their wing, nor could I properly appreciate their dusky greyness in the poor light conditions. We had driven over two hours to see birds that were a fatter version of the waxwings we see in Toronto parks regularly, and though I still admired their crests, I didn't get what all the fuss was about. And then, before I could give the backlit birds another chance, as if on cue from their conductor, the entire museum of Bohemian waxwings flew off.

I haven't seen a Bohemian waxwing since that day in early 2012. Every winter, I do everything I can to put myself in their flight path: I drive country roads north of the city where they've recently been seen, I scan every flock of cedar waxwings for a chunkier specimen among them, I obsess over eBird lists, and send frantic messages to birder friends on Twitter, begging for a heads-up. Every year, I miss them.

So my new nemesis bird is one I've seen already. But I saw it before I was ready, before I had the vocabulary to fully appreciate it. It's like trying to read Dante in the original when you've only had a year of basic Italian. I had no idea just how nomadic these flocks of birds can be. To me, the birds have a ghostly presence: they appear en masse, uttering faint, high-pitched trills as they fly, and then alight silently on a branch, devour all the fruit in their midst, rest briefly, and abscond in search of more food.

These unpredictable fruit connoisseurs are impossible to track down with certainty, and that's part of their charm. No longer a "fatter version of a cedar waxwing" in my mind, the ethereal Bohemian has risen to mythological proportions; every winter I pine for the bird's ingenious colour palette and wonder why more interior designers don't follow the Bohemian waxwing's lead. Is there anything more sophisticated than the way the bird's peachy facial blush, offset by a glistening black eye mask, contrasts with its silky grey back and finds an unexpected echo in the bronze undertail feathers?

I contemplated cancelling work commitments and hopping in the car earlier this winter, the day Monika texted me that she had just seen a tree-full of them in Guelph, but apart from the fact that the birds would likely be gone by the time I battled Toronto's rush-hour traffic, I feared that finally seeing this nemesis bird again would efface one of the last memories I have of birding with my friend Lucy. I can still see her, shivering, binoculars pointed at the tree of waxwings, staring up at the birds, sighing quietly to herself, and smiling as she tried to capture that moment, in all of its fragile detail, forever.

Bravery School

IT TOOK ME NEARLY FOUR YEARS OF VOLUNTEERING AT Tommy Thompson Park Bird Research Station to actually touch a bird. I had been waking up at 4:00 a.m. once a week during the spring and fall migration monitoring seasons, driving to the bird banding station and participating in their six-hour protocol without handling the birds directly. Everybody else volunteering at the station was there because they love to hold birds in the hand. They were biology and zoology students hoping for a career in ornithology, former fieldworkers nostalgic for their outdoorsy past, and teachers, retirees, vet technicians, nature store owners and enthusiasts from all over the world who wanted to add species to their list of banded birds—or, in banding-station-speak, to amass ticks. And then there was me.

I participated in the station-opening ritual, which included unfurling twenty-odd mist nets. Afterwards, I accompanied people on the half-hour net checks, and I watched as they extracted tangled birds from the nearly invisible nylon nets. First, you splay out the net and look for an opening, to determine how the bird has flown in; from there, you grab the bird's feet and disentangle them from the netting, which sometimes feels like giving the bird a pedicure. All being well, you delicately shimmy one wing out of the netting, then the other, and finally pluck the excess string over the bird's head—et voila! You've extracted a bird. In any one of those steps, a million things can go wrong, and the bird can be contorted in a variety of positions. Sometimes a bird can bounce out of one shelf of the net into another and end up double-bagged; sometimes the bird's tongue gets caught on the netting; sometimes the wings are pulled so tightly together it feels like the bird is wearing a backpack; sometimes you think you're making progress and the bird just gets more and more entangled. Extracting a bird from a mist net presents a topographical puzzle that requires not only prodigious dexterity, but also a dose of radical empathy that enables you to think from a bird's perspective, and a non-negligible measure of ESP to determine exactly how the bird flew into the net and the way it subsequently tangled itself in the net. It's part technique and part sixth sense.

I'm not exactly known for my manual dexterity. Or my puzzle-solving skills.

"I'm largely afraid of most living animals. Except for the odd human," I told my new friend at the banding station, a twenty-one-year-old master's student in evolutionary biology named Bronwyn. She had been volunteering at the station since she was fifteen and her fingers were so nimble that she could extract anything. During my first season, when I followed people to the nets and stood by, holding in my breath while they performed their careful extractions, I watched her remove everything from a ruby-throated hummingbird to a Cooper's hawk. She even untangled dragonflies without hurting them.

"So what are you doing here?"

It was a reasonable question. And I gave the only answer I had: "I'm overcoming fears."

At the banding station, I started out afraid of everything: afraid to furl the nets, afraid to untangle the birds. But most of all I was scared of hurting the birds. I'm a clumsy person by nature and have horrible flashbacks of accidentally hitting my sister in the face with a badminton racket when I was twelve and kicking a soccer ball into the neighbour's yard, only to have it collide with their three-year-old's face. My track record is not exactly golden. There are so many things that can go awry when extracting a bird from a net that for the first four years of volunteering at the banding station, I rarely attempted it.

Instead, I scribed. I sat in front of the data collection sheets, next to the person banding, and recorded all the information about a given bird. It's a privileged position, because you see every single bird that comes through the station, but also one that nobody really wants because you don't actually handle the birds.

Two years after I'd started volunteering, in one of my rare attempts to extract a bird, I broke a ruby-crowned kinglet's leg. I freed the first leg within seconds, but the second leg wouldn't give. Imagine holding a bird just shy of six grams by the feet, trying to unravel the netting from its toothpick legs, scraping the netting off its foot unsuccessfully, once, twice, three times, and then tugging a little. I heard the crack before I saw it, a limp swaying morsel, no longer gripping anything, no longer at a ninety-degree angle. I don't remember if the bird screeched or not—some birds are quiet through the process, some close their eyes and play dead, some yelp and bite—but I remember the snap of that leg breaking.

I immediately radioed Nigel, the master bander, who ran over, finished extracting the bird and let it go. He reassured me that birds could still fly, even with a broken leg.

"It happens," he said. But it took me two years to touch another bird.

When I watched my friend Charlotte extract birds, she warned, "There will be a time when you accidentally hurt a bird. It's awful and it happens." I kept hearing her words in my mind, but I couldn't reconcile that with what had actually happened. I'm not one to let things go. I thought twice about returning to the banding station after that. I even saw the kinglet's leg as confirmation of my worst fear: that if I had had a child, I would have been an unfit mother.

That sentence is entirely in the conditional mood. The fact of the matter was that I couldn't have children. My husband and I had tried and tried and then stopped trying after a year and a half of unsuccessful procedures at the fertility clinic, which left us equal parts exhausted, depressed and devastated. But the truer fact, the one I fear acknowledging even to myself, is that I've always been ambivalent about becoming a mother. And if I'm even more honest, which is to say, if I'm forced to admit something I've not even told my own mother, it's that I breathed an infinitesimal sigh of relief when we abandoned the fertility treatments. At least now I wouldn't have to live with the fear of finding out what kind of mother I'd be.

But the scribing was safe. I knew how to write, and I wasn't afraid of pencils breaking. I was even unafraid to make mistakes. I knew my place and found the process comforting. I saw every single bird. I watched as the bander blew on a bird's breast feathers to expose pinkish-yellow fat stores, and the occasional brood patch or X-rated cloacal protuberance. I wrote down the alphabetic code, the species name, the net from which we extracted it, the bird's sex and age, the time of extraction and the fat score. Sometimes I helped with an ID. I became a proficient scribe and once, during a particularly busy, chaotic day when we were overwhelmed with birds, I found myself scribing for four bird banders at once, all of whom shouted out numbers and codes to me. I knew what to listen for, knew what information to inscribe where, knew which bird belonged to whose voice.

I memorized bird codes, which usually included the first two letters of the first and second word of the bird's common name: AMRO for American robin, YEWA for yellow warbler, and so on. When a bird's common name is only one word, then the alpha code consists of its first four letters: VEER for veery, the unforgettable DICK for dickcissel and KILL for killdeer. To avoid alpha code repetition, some codes are harder to remember than others: BTNW for black-throated green warbler. It's now hard for me to think of a grey-headed catbird by any other name than a GRCA.

I didn't think my scribing was a skill until I watched other people perform the task with difficulty.

I COULDN'T STOP THINKING ABOUT THE CRACK OF THE KING-let's leg, the feel of the bird in my hand.

A few months later, I signed myself up for bravery school. Not literally, but close. I enrolled in an adult ballet class at the National Ballet School. A class in a professional dance studio with floor-to-ceiling mirrors, a barre and nowhere to hide. I had hesitated for two years before signing up for an "introduction to ballet" class—not on account of the price or the technical difficulty of the class, or the reality that, as an adult learner, I'd never achieve any sort of mastery, or that my body's inflexibility would likely prevent me from doing the simplest of moves, but on account of the mirrors.

The architecture of a dance studio is deliberately minimalistic and austere, so as not to draw attention to itself: high ceilings, a barre along three of the four walls, and enormous, all-seeing mirrors. The attention rests on the bodies in the centre of the room and the physical pyrotechnics they produce. The drama, the technical prowess, the grace—all from an assemblage of rounded arms, stretched legs, pointed toes, centred eyes, crowns of heads reaching upward, backs so straight one can almost sense the space between the vertebrae.

I'd been there before and it had been a disaster. "I'm here to reclaim my childhood," I told my teacher when he asked about our reasons for signing up for the class. I remembered the five positions, but I had forgotten about the predominance of French. As we did tendus and were instructed to point our foot *à la seconde*, or *en croix*, I knew what my teacher meant even before he demonstrated. I had begun learning French and ballet at roughly the same time, though neither one had been my choice. By my early thirties, I had abandoned both of them for good.

And yet, when my teacher said *plié*, I didn't think of walking down rainy Parisian streets alone, a dissertation not completed, a marriage drained of its energy. Instead, I focused on lengthening my core, on looking ahead, my eyes slightly raised, and gently, slowly descending into a bent-knee position. I had never thought of the meaning of the word *plié*: to fold. Yet here I was, folding my past lives into my present one, my childhood fears, my slouching back, my disastrous first marriage, into this purely technical moment, thighs turned out, sternum open, folding and meeting the world on my own terms, spine lengthening, my body performing a new act.

WHEN MY GRANDMOTHER ARRIVED IN CANADA IN 1987, SHE may well have expected her granddaughter, whom she hadn't seen in nine years, to resemble a younger version of Maya Plisetskaya, feet turned out, head resting high on her shoulders, a twelve-year-old about to break into a petit allegro combination with a chassé or an arabesque. After all, she had stood in line for hours to buy me biographies of famous ballerinas, and before I could do a *rond de jambe* I could recite the life trajectories of Galina Ulanova, Anna Pavlova and Tamara Karsavina. Instead, there I was, waiting to greet her at the airport—hair poorly combed, hiding my slouching back in a baggy sweater that rested atop a blue tube skirt, arms hanging limp by my sides.

What my letters to my grandmother in clumsy Cyrillic script neglected to mention was that I couldn't stand ballet. I quit as soon as I turned nine. My parents' decision to enroll their daughter in Vancouver's elite ballet school—stemming from a combination of their own belief that one should learn an art form from its most rigorous practitioners and an earnest desire to correct my horrible posture—backfired. Due to my inflexibility and incredible lack of grace, my teachers refused to allow me to advance to the next level. For four years, I repeated the introductory class, and by the time I quit, I was more than a head taller than all the five-year-olds and still the least pliable one in the room.

I once tried, against my teacher's advice, to join my own age group, but they were already doing the splits, their *grand battements* high, their *cou-de-pied* in *relevé* held with precision, their positions polished. Their hair slicked back and buns held firmly in place with bobby pins, they did formations in the middle of the room, their heads all tilted in the same direction. I slouched, my hair a perpetual mess; since my parents taught piano on Saturdays, there was nobody to put my hair in a bun, and I got a ride with my father's middle-aged piano student named George, who taught ESL, had six offspring of his own whom he'd abandoned, wore an undershirt instead of a button-down and always sported a straw hat. He was in no position to offer coiffure assistance. And so I collected my mop of hair into a lopsided ponytail, put on my short-sleeved blue leotard, tights crumpled and dirty at the ankles because I never quite got the foot position right, and settled into my slightly oversized ballet slippers. Always buy a size bigger, my mother reasoned, to ensure that I'd have something to grow into; my closet held a collection of shoes one to three sizes bigger than what I wore at the time. I could divine my future just by examining my wardrobe.

"How will you fix your back now?" my grandmother lamented. "If only you'd stuck with it, tried harder, practised more."

"I just didn't like it." I wanted to tell her I wasn't ballet material. None of the ballerinas in the books she sent me had my body type; none of them slouched, couldn't touch their toes or fell straight to the floor like I did when everyone else in class cartwheeled across the gymnasium.

"You threw away an opportunity." But what she meant was this: *I too wanted to dance and might have, had it not been for the war and our evacuation from Odessa to Fergana in 1941, where we lived eight to a room, our bread rationed to two slices a day, and where pirouettes from fifth position were the furthest thing from my mind.*

I will never dance in front of an audience, but every week I stand at the barre and recover a piece of my childhood, and my grandmother's, as I patiently work on my turnout, and kick my legs upward, to the side and back for *grand battements*. Mine remain clunky, hardly grand—my hips not quite in alignment, my feet turned out only ninety degrees, my fifth position much like my third, my back still far from the version of itself I would like to inhabit. Occasionally I steal a glance in the mirror and see a person performing a *port de bras*, her *relevé* shaky but tenacious—and there, looking back at me, unexpectedly, my body offers me a glimmer of grace.

AFTER A YEAR OF FORCING MYSELF TO LOOK IN THE MIRROR, to accept the limitations of my body, I found myself ready to return to the mist nets. Make no mistake, I am no extractor extraordinaire, nor do I aspire to that. I will likely always make net rounds with a radio in my pocket and will more than likely always call for assistance for every fourth bird or so. But two springs ago, I attempted a black-and-white warbler extraction that worked: once I firmly had the feet in my hands, I opened the bird's wing, shimmied it out of the netting, then freed the other wing, and just as I had started to sweat at the thought of having to untangle the bird's head from the net, just as my brain immediately went to replay the sound of the kinglet's leg cracking on an endless loop, just when I was about to radio Nigel for help, I took a deep breath, moved the netting to one side, then the other, until it started to give a little, and then with one swooping motion lifted the net over the bird's head and bill, and, just like that, the bird was free.

And there I stood, in the middle of a red-ant-infested trail, a mosquito buzzing beside my cheek, holding a freshly extracted eight-gram, male black-and-white warbler in my hand. I gently placed him in a cloth bag and walked back to the banding station, where I would inscribe his data into the register.

Seeing myself in the ballet studio mirror still often inspires horror, or makes me wish I could trade my body for a better, straighter, more proficient version. But forcing myself to look in the mirror has been an exercise in bravery. I'll probably always be able to feel that kinglet's leg snapping in my hand, but with every bird I extract, the memory of the cracked bone becomes a little dimmer.

The Wanderer

ANYBODY ELSE WOULD HAVE CONSIDERED THE ESCAPADE crazy. A spotted towhee had lost its way and had ended up in the hamlet of Glen Williams, just northwest of Toronto. Though I had checked the road conditions and had concluded that driving north along icy and snowy roads in mid-January would be madness, I went anyhow. I went without telling my husband exactly where we'd be travelling. I went while trying very hard to excise the weather report from my memory.

One begins amassing a life list at some point shortly after birding becomes something that one dreams about constantly. Initially the list has a wild growth spurt, but things slow down considerably once one has faithfully birded a particular area for a couple of years. By *faithfully* I mean every Saturday, rain or shine. I mean returning to the same places over and over again until you've memorized who likes to perch on which trees. After four years of birding at Earl Bales Park, a ten-minute drive from my house, I could show you the northern flicker's favourite hangouts; I could take you to the tree where the northern parula likes to perch and sing his heart out every spring; I could let you stand in front of the trees where the palm warbler makes his first appearance and where the black-and-white warbler creeps headfirst down the tree, performing his classic nuthatch impersonation. I could also show you the tree where I mistook the rattle of a red squirrel for an exotic kingfisher.

And so, when a rarity appears on the horizon, one doesn't wait. One hops in the car regardless of the weather and heads for the bird, because one clearly knows a birding truism: birds have their own agenda and operate on their own time. They will not wait for you to get your act together. They may very well be one-day wonders.

I will not hide the fact that a part of me wanted to see the spotted towhee in order to add another bird to my life list. But a greater part of me wanted to see what a western bird looked like when displaced in eastern Canada. Spotted towhees are California natives, and I wondered whether this one had ever seen snow and how it felt beneath his feet, for a bird who is so used to the alternating mossy, coastal moisture and piercing inland heat of the California landscape. My years on the west coast didn't expose me to ski country, and I had all but forgotten that the towhee might also have been entirely at home in snow.

Most of all, I wanted to see the vagrant spotted towhee because I too had once been out of my element entirely.

I ARRIVED IN MISSOURI IN 2005, ALREADY HAVING AMASSED everything I needed: an excellent job in my field, an apartment overlooking a former-railway-turned-recreational-trail, a car. The town with "one of everything" charmed me during my interview and slowly began to undo me once I began the work of chiselling it into a home. I searched for a mate at every turn—online, at departmental gatherings, at new faculty retreats, in yoga classes, at farmer's markets, in pottery classes, on cycling escapades. The only explanation for my predicament was that I had become a victim of the whims of geographic error.

A WISER PERSON MIGHT HAVE PAUSED AT THE THREE-CAR accident on the highway and possibly turned back; I chose to ignore it and sped toward my bird group meeting. I hadn't planned on going birding in the midst of January flurries and limited visibility. I, who berates my husband for his inability to moderate his workouts at the gym, who parades such lofty phrases as "I would never put myself in danger," jumped into my car, which was sans snow tires.

Brete, Heather and I were on the road at 7:00 a.m. in the mid-January darkness, hopeful that we'd have a new bird to add to our Ontario lists and possibly our life lists. But I was after something else too. A sense of recognition. How does a spotted towhee—an unexpected vagrant visitor from the west—find himself in southern Ontario? A miscalculation of weather, perhaps, or a momentary lapse in judgment or a misreading of the lay of the land? Either way, I'd been there.

NO MATTER HOW HARD I TRIED, MISSOURI'S VERNACULAR remained slightly beyond my reach. "You're not from here, are you…" My Pilates instructor had phrased it with certainty; my dental hygienist had added a question mark to the end; my car mechanic had said the words apologetically; my car salesman shook his head, as if to blame me for my provenance; and my students didn't need to say it, they just knew. The closest I could come to explaining my situation was an image of interminable sky that reminded me I was not of this place. It witnessed my fruitless attempts at dating and my daily return to a comfortable apartment with bare walls that I had no desire to decorate.

I tried my luck with JDate, in the hope of meeting someone from a shared cultural background. I went on dates with other tortured academics, including a psychologist who grew up with a domineering mother he couldn't stop talking about, and various Russian-Jewish consultants who wore the requisite black leather jackets and ultimately determined that I was neither Russian nor Jewish enough for them. When I tried eHarmony, an e-mail informed me that they didn't have a single match for me within a two-hundred-mile radius.

All the while, my great-grandmother's mantra lurked in the back of my mind: "The way to a man's heart is through his stomach," which I loosely translated as "You'll never meet a decent man until you learn to cook." On the recommendation of a friend who understood my predicament, I ordered Mark Bittman's *How to Cook Everything*. Were my great-grandmother still alive, she would have concluded that, at the age of thirty-one, I'd already run out of time.

Under Bittman's tutelage I learned how to knead dough for baguettes. He told me how much pressure to apply, which muscles to flex, how to probe the sticky texture with my knuckles. I repeated the incantatory rhythm of his imperative verbs. *Beat, pulse, stir, mash.* When my phone didn't ring or my e-mail inbox was empty, I turned to Bittman's oracular presence. I devoured lessons in washing and slicing leeks efficiently, made mental notes about the proper way to roast and carve a chicken.

I superimposed my upbringing on Bittman's and began to see him as a child of displaced immigrant Jews, wanderers attempting to read logic into our culinary heritage. He might have had a mother, like mine, whose elaborate meals became her only chance at conversation with family members she doubted she'd ever see again. He would understand my mother's impulse, as a twenty-six-year-old immigrant recently transplanted to Edmonton and immersed in a language she could barely decipher, to study family recipes that she had neatly transcribed on graph paper. Her recipes offered a momentary escape, a breath of fried-onion-infused air straight from her grandmother's kitchen in Odessa.

And yet my kitchen boasted more appliances than food. My piano and bookshelves no longer soothed me. I even found myself developing a crush on Bob Costas during the Winter Olympics of 2006. His head of dyed hair greeted me every morning for two weeks, and before long I found myself reading his Wikipedia biography, learning that he was Greek-American and deciding that since my Cyrillic alphabet had derived from Greek script, we were made for one another.

I WANDERED FROM ORGANIC CHESTNUT ROASTS TO CYCLING, to pottery classes, to walks along the Katy Trail, all the while hoping for a better understanding of *here*. For the first time since my year in Vancouver, I became a serial enthusiast, taste-testing one hobby after another. I tried regular yoga and Pilates classes, joined a Slow Food chapter, developed a taste for BBQ; I contemplated buying a smoker for the not-so-distant future in which I would likely meet someone who qualified as husband material and we would buy a quaint professorville bungalow.

I even bought a bicycle and joined a low-intensity cycling group called the Sleazys, short for "Slow and Easy." In fact, they turned out to be neither. Our rides were forty kilometres, over rolling hills. The kind people in the group sandwiched me between them to protect me from wind and to offer the requisite push when I might require it. My first few rides were agonizing. I couldn't keep up with the group, I had trouble breathing, my thighs burned. To pass the time and forget my pain, I grilled my seventy-something spandex-clad mentor, Bob, about his seven children until he laughed and admitted he'd forgotten what child number five did for a living. Bob's sturdy frame shielded me from the wind and he occasionally helped push me up a hill without ever asking if I needed the assistance. After talking to Bob, I moved on to Charlie, who rode with his toes pointed outward, like first position in ballet class, and pedalled effortlessly. He focused his glance straight ahead and wasn't interested in small talk. When I realized I couldn't keep up with him, I rode at the back of the pack with Brenda, who told me about her kohlrabi plants and offered to bring me cilantro next time we met. I waved to the passing pickup trucks, shot a beaming smile to the bikers riding on the other side of the road, and didn't recognize myself.

I was learning how to shift gears, feeling muscles in my legs that I had only heard of or seen in magazines. I decided that next week I'd take the plunge and buy bike shorts. I sprinted up toward Charlie and tried to engage him in conversation, only to realize that he was monosyllabic; I let him whiz by me. I wondered why the group was called "Slow and Easy," since I was riding faster than I thought possible, and I hadn't yet learned to utter *easy* and *cycling* in the same breath. Breathing heavily, I was back to garden talk with Brenda, though I didn't understand a word. Hygrometers, high shade, tilling techniques, biennials, halophytes, mulching, nitrogen monitoring. I nodded, resorting to vestiges of ancient Greek and Latin to interpret her terminology.

An unexpected sunset interrupted Brenda's endless monologue on summer tomatoes and I was momentarily stunned by the burning red patch over the empty field to my left. I barely had time to inhale and the intensity began to bleed out horizontally, invading the sky above the field. I knew the sunset would be gone when we reached the parking lot.

For a moment I wondered how it was that Missouri had rendered me speechless, my breath suspended. The first time I travelled to Rome, I couldn't describe the place; I walked the city in a daze that lasted for the better part of a week. The architecture had robbed me of my ability to form logical thoughts. Years later, I read an essay by Stendhal about a similar experience, which he called the *Syndrome de Florence*: when faced with describing physical surroundings that are so visually arresting, one is stunned, rendered speechless or even physically incapacitated, and sometimes, literally, falls ill. Somehow knowing that my exposure to Roman ruins had literary pedigree made my speechlessness easier to bear.

I had discovered a Missouri syndrome. Every time I got on my bicycle, it transported me elsewhere. Through my fatigue, I managed to see the place anew. Maybe my emotions were heightened, maybe I was drugged by the endorphins, but my surroundings came to life. For those brief moments, I didn't long to escape.

THAT DAY IN JANUARY ON MY WAY TO THE SPOTTED TOWHEE, what I wanted was a low-grade Toronto syndrome. I wasn't interested in something that would render me physically incapacitated or ill (and besides, who am I kidding, Toronto is no place for the sublime); instead, I wanted something that would give me glimpses, glimmers, of surprise, transporting me away from the mundane, adding something to my life.

I wanted to stop running. My whole life I had been itinerant. Running toward something, running away from something or someone. I moved almost every year and became an expert in packing my bags, loading up the car and heading off.

I wanted a reason to stay.

A VAGRANT ADDS PIQUANCY TO BIRDING. IT'S THE unexpected, the unprecedented, the magic of the new. As birders, we chase after what is unusual. So often we forget that for the bird, the experience is disorienting, a loss of familiar surroundings, being blown off course in a perilous journey. Vagrants very rarely survive. They're wired for elsewhere. And so there's a touch of transgression in our chase. We're after the very thing that shouldn't be: the accident of nature.

When we arrive at the farmhouse in Glen Williams, we scope the territory. On the ground next to the front door, next to a fat mourning dove, there he is, a loner of a bird that mostly resembles his eastern counterpart, but imperfectly. The mourning dove eyes him with suspicion, sensing something unusual in the gleaming black head with a brilliant red eye and a mix of white stripes and polka-dots on its wings. He's out of place no matter how hard he tries to commune with the tree sparrows. I watch him hop about, feasting on seeds, perhaps wondering how it is that life brought him to this place he never knew existed.

I wanted to tell this misplaced avian stranger, whose accent and demeanour are just slightly other, that I've been there, that I understand. Sometimes, I wanted to say, the home you end up making for yourself isn't anything like you could have divined, and before you know it you're living amidst a cacophonic assortment of birds and elephants, with a person whose habits and interests are alien to you, and, perhaps strangest of all, you're standing in the snow, staring at a vagrant bird with a group of people who have now become akin to a second family, and yet somehow, in the midst of this unimaginable present, you are at home.

The Big Hummingbird

I AM A SPECIALIST IN MISIDENTIFICATION. I'M GETTING BET-ter, and I will continue to improve as long as I bird, but I still make mistakes constantly. The only way to improve as a birder is through experience, and experience equals hours spent in the field looking, identifying, questioning your identification, misidentifying, doubling back and correcting yourself, and then comparing that particular sighting to others you've seen and recognizing the different posture, different light.

When I first started birding, I was ashamed of my mistakes. After the initial rapid accumulation of knowledge comes the frustration. The more you know, the more you realize you don't know (and you'll probably never know). As soon as I felt comfortable with the bay-breasted warbler, I had to contend with the fact that not only did the female differ drastically from the male, but a bay-breasted in breeding plumage looks nothing like the exact same warbler four months later. Male songbirds are at their most colourful in the spring, when they're desperate to attract a mate; by the time fall rolls around, most of them moult into a much duller-looking outfit because by fall, when they're beginning their journeys southward, there's nobody left to impress. Breeding has already taken place, the torch has been passed on, and the only job of a bay-breasted warbler is to fatten up so that he can reach Central America and rest up for the winter. Not only that, but by fall, the usually chestnut-and-black-headed bird becomes a bland greenish-greyish item virtually indistinguishable from the blackpoll warbler, who sported a black cap and a black-and-white striped number in the spring.

With those warblers, failure is understandable. But there are times when your failures are so perplexing that you wonder what it is you've been doing all this time.

I had been birding for five years the day I looked up high in a tree at Long Point Provincial Park and saw something that looked familiar.

"It's a hummingbird! A really big one, for some reason."

"Which way are you looking?" Brete asked.

"Up there in that tree with green leaves. The bird is near the top, on a branch. God, I've never seen such a gargantuan hummingbird. I think their bills are usually pointier." I stuck to my ID, though. I could swear the bird vibrated in that bumble-bee way hummingbirds usually do.

"Julia, what I'm seeing up here is a green heron."

"You're kidding me." I put my binoculars down. Confusing a green heron with a hummingbird is like confusing an elephant with a marmot. What had I seen, exactly, and how could I make such an egregious mistake that it sounded like I'd become deranged? A green heron was the size of at least 150 hummingbirds. I felt nauseated.

"Well, I'm not quite sure how you saw a hummer up there, but sometimes size plays tricks on us." Brete, ever the pedagogue, tried hard not to ridicule me.

"Do green herons often hang out in trees?" Still trying to redeem myself.

"Yes. They nest there."

There was no way to undo my idiotic mistake. It wasn't just my bird group that heard me. This was peak spring migration and dozens of people had witnessed my identification skills in action.

There was nothing to do but keep birding. It was even worse than the time I called out a Canada warbler on the Tulip Tree Trail at Rondeau Provincial Park. Ten people proceeded to photograph the bird until someone tapped my shoulder and gently corrected me: "Actually, it's a maggie." Short for magnolia warbler.

Every time I call out an ID, I follow it up with, "But I'm usually wrong about most things," largely to avoid a repeat of the Canada warbler moment.

It's hard to measure my birding progress. Ten years later, I am no longer a complete neophyte. I can follow along with a birdy conversation, I have less trouble absorbing ornithology lectures than I did when I first joined the Toronto Ornithological Club, and I can offer great contributions in the bird-home-decorating-kitsch department. I also keep up with most birding books written for a general audience. But I know I'm still far from being a skilled birder.

Maybe the point isn't about measuring at all; it's about seeing. Who cares if I'm still not the first one to call out an ID, or if I call out a wrong one, or if I still need professional help finding the more elusive specimens? Before birds, most things I did were measured for success: tests, essays, a completed dissertation, job applications. But with birds, there is no barometer for success beyond my own personal enjoyment. I'm not in it for the science, I'm not in it for the competitive aspect, I'm not in it for the thrill of garnering an extensive life list. Too old to be a precocious birder, too little scientific knowledge to contribute to the ornithological conversation.

So what have I been doing, exactly? Learning to look. Learning to befriend failure. The peculiar thing about my love affair with birds is that nobody cares about it but me. There is no external assessment. Every Saturday, my parents ask me what I've seen, but they rarely listen to my response. Leon patiently lets me show him field-guide pictures of the amazing bird I've just seen or the even more amazing bird I just failed to see, but he doesn't care whether I've seen one bird or 150.

I used to be nervous whenever I took him with me on a bird walk. I wanted to prove to him that I'm a Birding Success Story. Once, in Washington, DC, I tried to impress him with multiple tufted titmouse sightings and a secretive winter wren that I was proud to be able to locate. I showed him an eastern towhee and couldn't resist telling him about the bird's "drink-your-tea" song, which left Leon cold.

"What's that brown spot in the tree?" Leon asked.

"Probably a squirrel's nest," I said, but just in case, I raised my binoculars to check. "Uh...it's not a nest."

"What is it?"

"A fucking barred owl!" I shouted. "You found an owl!"

We ran up the hill behind the trees to get a better angle on the owl, and I found myself equal parts thrilled and annoyed that I hadn't been the one to find the bird.

How could Leon, who refuses to use binoculars because he prides himself on being the best Naked-Eye Birder in Ontario, actually find the bird of the day? Forget day, it was the bird of our entire week-long trip. I'd seen barred owls before, but I had never been the one to find the bird. This one was particularly photogenic and regaled us with multiple 280-degree neck-twists. Then, exhausted from his overexertion, he sat there dozing, with one eye open, letting us watch him until we'd had our fill.

Leon reminded me that he'd seen the lone bald eagle too, and he was right. Not only that, but he also spotted a regal-looking red-tailed hawk sitting on a branch, quietly surveying potential prey. And a hermit thrush, which would have been no big deal, but it was my FOY (first of the year) and that fact alone irked me. I'd long had a vision of us birding together in his retirement, but what if he ended up being better than me? Leon is infinitely more meticulous than I am and, I worried, his future as a potential bird-watcher was clearly more viable than mine. Maybe birding together would do more harm than good for our relationship, I thought to myself.

This was eight years into our marriage, and my husband was well versed in interpreting my silences—and especially my dejected posture, when I walk with my head down, my binoculars draped over one shoulder.

"Thanks for showing me the tufted bird and that other singing one."

"But I'm not the one who found the owl." I hadn't wanted to say it; the words just came out.

He put his arm around my slumped shoulders. "Do you really think I care how many birds you find? I wouldn't have even known that was an owl if you hadn't told me.

I just look for blobs in trees. It's what you always ask me to do."

It's true. Whenever we go outside, no matter where we are, I instruct him to watch for movement everywhere and look for clumps in trees and on utility poles. It's not his fault that he happens to be very good at it. I squeezed out a smile and reached for his hand.

ON OUR LAST DAY IN DC, MARTHA TEXTED ME THAT A VIRGINIA rail had appeared at Colonel Samuel Smith Park in Toronto. "It'll probably still be there when you get back," she said. Once back, I checked eBird, and everybody who'd seen the bird unanimously said the rail was right next to a culvert, walking around in the reeds. At seven o'clock on the morning after we arrived home, I decided to drive out to the park. The only problem, I realized as I navigated the morning rush hour, was that I had forgotten to look up "culvert" in the dictionary and actually had no idea where in the park this bird could be.

As I drove in stop-and-go traffic, I did exactly what I promised my husband I would never do while driving: I dialed Martha's phone number on my cell.

"Martha! It's Julia," I always forget that I don't have to self-identify on a message machine, since my name pops up in her missed calls list. "I'm on my way to get the rail, but I actually don't know what a culvert is. Call me or text, please."

Martha is a librarian with a better vocabulary than mine and, as it turns out, a son who was obsessed with culverts as a small child. Once I knew to look for an enormous pipe pumping water into a small pond, I felt a bit better about my escapade. Martha sent directions, too, but in a fit of disorientation I walked the wrong way, found a culvert and waited. I saw three mallards and a gadwall. No Virginia rail, which shouldn't be a huge surprise. Rails are notoriously skittish and I'd only seen one once before. It had been found for me by Brete. I wondered where all the birders were. Two days ago, birder-paparazzi were all over the rail.

Finally I saw someone with binoculars. "I'm trying to find the rail. Have you seen it?" I asked.

"I did see it yesterday. But if you wait here you might never see it. It's by the big culvert right next to the parking lot. I'll show you where I saw it yesterday, if you want."

"I'm so glad I ran into you!" I'm obviously no culvert expert.

We arrived at the right place. And I waited. I actually got down and looked inside the culvert, in case the bird was lurking there. In vain. "A waiting game," the friendly gentleman with the binoculars warned me. I checked every single reed and waited for close to an hour before I decided to go and buy a coffee, only to realize that I had forgotten my wallet at home, which brought my rail quest to a definitive halt. I said goodbye to friendly Mr. Binoculars, who was by now sitting on the culvert, his legs dangling on either side, a long-lensed camera pointed toward a duck. "A blue-winged teal," he said.

I tried to muster a smile, but it's hard to get excited about a teal when you have rails on your mind. The weather forecast for the next two days called for freezing rain, which I doubted the rail could withstand, and as I drove home in the thick of rush hour, I bemoaned the fact that I had failed to see the rail on account of such prosaic stupidity.

When I finally found the rail three days later, I shouted so loudly that I almost frightened the bird. By some miracle, he had survived the ice storm that more or less paralyzed southern Ontario. I watched him dart in and out of the reeds, where his entire body, except for his bright red bill, was perfectly camouflaged with the tall grasses. And then I caught him at just the right angle, and he posed for me, long enough for me to feel like we were developing a relationship of sorts, that he understood my needs and anxieties, and knew that seeing him had required hard work and persistence on my part, and that he, a peculiar marsh bird that looked a bit like a chicken, depending on the angle, was, at that moment, the loveliest bird I had ever laid eyes on.

Not Even a Rock Pigeon

THE KIWANIS MUSIC COMPETITION WAS AN ANNUAL ORDEAL that I endured as a child. Each year, the adjudicators came to a consensus that both my technique and my musicality needed work, that I was perhaps too tentative in my interpretations and that I could stand to look a little happier when I performed. Each year, I didn't quite measure up to the rest of my parents' piano students. Most often, I came in fourth out of six contestants, and the ones who ranked behind me were either no-shows or had failed to memorize their piece to the end. Perhaps it was the adjudicators' gracious way of letting me know that my playing almost measured up to the top three, who received certificates, but that in reality the gulf between me and the third place winner was vast.

I KNEW THE GREAT CANADIAN BIRDATHON, ORGANIZED BY Bird Studies Canada, would be different. Still, I worried. Would I measure up? Would I expose the gaps in my birding knowledge? Would I look like a fraud? It sounded like an insane undertaking: see as many birds as you can within any region you choose in a twenty-four-hour period. Drive yourself into the ground with the sole goal of amassing as many species as you can and possibly beating last year's total. Stranger still, in a birdathon, the teams aren't necessarily competing against anyone, since there are neither winners nor judges and the entire thing operates on an honour system.

"What do you get at the end?" I asked Brete. I still operated in a reward-system mentality.

"The goal is to raise money for conservation."

"No, but at the end of the gruelling day, what do you get?"

It would take a few years for me to discover that the point of a birdathon was...the birds. Even numbers, and the actual counting, were far less important than the process of finding them.

I read three of Brete's reports from past birdathons before deciding to participate. Initially the reports read like a transcription of a delirious, verging on masochistic, twenty-four-hour quest for the holy grail, consisting of elusive numbers and two nights in a motel. But five years into birding, I knew there was something to be said for spending an uninterrupted stretch of time engrossed in the process of searching. Mixed in with the repetitive pattern of looking and failing to see would, I knew, be startling moments of unforeseen joy. What tipped the scale was Brete's decision to include Point Pelee on the birdathon schedule. I had heard of this mythical place but had not yet been to the southernmost tip of the provincial park, where warblers were so tired from their migratory flight that they didn't even bother to fly into the trees; most of them were literally at your feet. I also wanted to see the spectacle that was Pelee. All those people in Tilley hats, with high-end optics, all engaged in the same pursuit of adding more migratory songbirds to their lists.

Hotels in Leamington, the nearest town to Point Pelee National Park, fill up a year in advance. Birders flock to Pelee from all over the world—it's one of the most reliable migration hubs with the largest quantity of colourful New World warblers. I had pitched an article about doing my first birdathon to *Maisonneuve* magazine and was now there, officially, on assignment.

BRETE'S ITINERARY HAD STRATEGIC WISDOM. WE WOULD visit three locations—Mitchell's Bay, Point Pelee and Rondeau Provincial Park—which he referred to as a "Golden Triangle," to guarantee a maximum number of species. To ensure that we'd be at Mitchell's Bay before sunrise, we reserved rooms in a cheap motel twenty-five minutes away, in Chatham, Ontario. My alarm went off at 4:00 a.m., and after a short stop for coffee, we were off. We arrived at our desired deserted concession road—chosen because a yellow-headed blackbird had been spotted there a few days earlier—while it was still dark. Brete called out at least a dozen birds he identified by song, and I was happy to contribute a correct yellow warbler song ID, the only one I contributed all morning.

As it grew light, we heard a creaky call that resembled a red-winged blackbird but was different enough to make an impression. And then I saw it: a Meyer-lemon-coloured head resting atop a slick black body, almost as if the bird's getup had been fashioned in a children's dress studio, where one child said to another, you make the head and I'll make the body.

I had attempted to see a yellow-headed blackbird once before, when I tried to pick it out amidst five thousand other blackbirds scurrying on the ground and flying low. I had only recently started birding at that point and was drawn by reports of the blackbird with the bright yellow head, something I could surely recognize. We scanned groupings of birds—mostly red-winged blackbirds, brown-headed cowbirds, common grackles—in search of the otherworldly yellow head, but the more we scanned the territory, the blacker everything looked. There wasn't even a hint of yellow. I spent the hour and a half staring into a sea of black, seemingly identical birds, dreaming of lunch.

But the birdathon didn't play out that way. There are some birding days where things fall into place. The bird you hope to see makes an appearance, as planned, and you revel in the miracle of it all. My attempts at scanning thousands of blackbirds, looking for the elusive golden head, only made the experience of seeing one all the more momentous. My teammates picked up about twenty-five birds by sound alone, while I stared in wonder at the screeching bird that looked like he was wearing a bumble-bee costume.

We arrived at Pelee just after 7:00 a.m., already on a high from spotting the hard-to-find blackbird. And it was just like in all the pictures I'd seen. Birders were everywhere, trading sightings, eyeing one another's optics with varying degrees of envy and respect. I thought I had a lot of birdy apparel, but it turned out my wardrobe was nothing compared with the people who came to Pelee. I saw hats decorated in bird pins, licence plates with birdy puns, scopes the likes of which I had only read about online. As

I fumbled with my field guide and held it between my legs while adjusting my binoculars, the multipocketed vests that I had once considered the epitome of bad taste now looked practical and I found myself entertaining the possibility of wearing one for the next birdathon. I heard French, German and Spanish spoken around me. I had been on bird walks with thirty people before, but I had never seen anything on this scale.

"Were there other people at that Pelee place when you did your birdathon?" my mother asked me the next day.

"Other people? It was like when Vladimir Horowitz came to Moscow. Remember the footage of hundreds of people lining up outside the conservatory?"

"That was a monumental event. A once-in-a-lifetime opportunity."

"Well that's how birders feel about warblers at Pelee. Even though most of them go every year."

IN 1985, VLADIMIR HOROWITZ WAS INVITED TO PERFORM A recital at the Moscow State Conservatory. It was his first visit to Russia since he had emigrated in 1921. The concert was broadcast live, and since we couldn't yet afford cable, we went to my parents' student's house at 9:00 a.m. to watch the broadcast of an evening concert, Moscow time. I sat on the floor in front of the TV screen, half-doing my homework, half-watching an old man with an effeminate silk kerchief play Mozart on an enormous grand piano, which he'd had shipped from New York. It surprised me that he barely moved his body as he played; instead, his flat fingers ran wild across the keyboard, in a controlled frenzy, eliciting sounds more delicate and dramatic than I'd heard before.

It wasn't just that my parents were seeing footage of Russia on TV for the first time since emigrating—this was really Russia, unlike the footage in *White Nights*, which was actually filmed in Finland—but that my father had studied with Horowitz's sister Regina for years. My parents couldn't take their eyes off the screen and even claimed to recognize a few audience members. My father had spent a semester studying at the Moscow Conservatory, and he narrated every scene. It wasn't just a concert; it was a homecoming. It also represented a slight loosening of Soviet regulations, a portent of the real family reunification my mother hoped for. By the end of the concert the stage lay submerged under a mountain of flowers—mainly carnations, the cut flower of choice in Soviet Russia—and Horowitz looked even smaller than he did at the piano. My parents were moved to tears. I was mostly happy that I got to miss my Sunday morning swimming lesson.

FOR SOME, PELEE IS A YEARLY RITUAL THAT NEVER DISAP-points. Although migration is fairly similar every year, it's never identical. One never knows what will turn up and one also never knows which birds one will miss. When I told people that I had developed an interest in birds, the first question was inevitably, "Have you been to Pelee?" Arriving at the park felt like the end of a pilgrimage. I had thought that the sight would feel exotic, but instead it felt comforting. I felt instantly at home.

With multiple bird walks happening at the same time, the place was swarming with people. Being at Pelee felt like attending a choir rehearsal where everybody sang a different part; people called out names of birds constantly and after a while I had no idea where to look. I'd like to experience Pelee when it's less crowded, but maybe part of the pleasure is the fact that it's overrun with people. Maybe the allure of Pelee is actually in the sight of so many birders.

We embarked on our warbler hunt in earnest. The parade of birds greeted us before we even stepped out of the tram leading to the tip of the peninsula. One more resplendent than the next, many of the birds were so exhausted after a night of non-stop flying that they hovered about on the ground, so co-operative that you'd think they were stopping for photo ops. The birds I'd studied all winter swarmed around me, and the names I had longed to pronounce aloud delighted me with their sound: Cape May, Blackburnian, Wilson's, northern parula, scarlet tanager, indigo bunting, Baltimore oriole, and yellow, bay-breasted and black-and-white warbler. I even caught a glimpse of my first ever hooded warbler, the skittish understorey-loving bright yellow bird who looks like he's clad in a black balaclava. By 11:00 a.m. we were close to eighty species, but already starting to race against the clock.

In a birdathon, time is of the essence, so we couldn't linger the way I wanted to. After a quick stop for lunch at a restaurant with plastic birds everywhere, we set out for the nearby Hillman Marsh Conservation Area, where there were fewer people. We picked up some ducks and our numbers grew to a respectable level; by this point we were nearing the hundred-species mark. At the marsh, I displayed my delinquent bird-song identification skills and mistook an ovenbird for a cardinal.

"Just think. A year ago you didn't even know an ovenbird existed," Heather said, always trying to be encouraging.

"Remember the 'teacher-teacher-teacher' mnemonic," Brete said. I wanted to tell him that I remembered just that, but accidentally confused it with the cardinal's song. Progress is incremental. So very much like life, this business of birding. "Don't underestimate the importance of persevering," he added.

From the marsh we drove to the Blenheim Sewage Lagoons to get some shorebirds and the usual bobolink that hangs out there along with the purple martins. From there we drove toward Rondeau Provincial Park and, while en route, up to a hamlet called Erieau, where we saw a most unlikely sight for the third weekend in May: a snowy owl in an entirely dry field.

Throughout the day, I kept track of our numbers on a piece of paper; I was used to scribing. The first hundred were easy to amass, but thereafter every single bird took work. By mid-afternoon we were exhausted and I questioned the point of what we were doing. Driving from hotspot to hotspot, accumulating sightings in order to... to what? We were raising money for conservation, sure, but was counting birds from morning till night really the best way to go about the enterprise? We didn't even have a chance to linger and take the birds in; we saw a dapper canvasback, but I didn't have time to delight in its dignified form—that unmistakable elongated rusty head, set atop a dazzling white body flanked by black neck and tail feathers.

I had never before spent a full day among birds. Our only responsibility on birdathon day is to see as many species as we can, without thinking of much else. It's an exercise in strategy, certainly, but also an exercise in managing disappointment and in thinking spontaneously and adjusting plans according to the birds. It's the only day of the year when I think of birds first, before thinking of myself. Food, sleep, everything else is secondary. It's also a day in which one forgets about the rest of life and lives for the birds. There's something selfless about it.

I couldn't sustain this rhythm for much longer than a day, but there's an adrenaline rush that accompanies a birdathon. You're racing against the clock and against your best number, trying to beat it. When the afternoon drew to a close, I surprised myself by not wanting to leave.

The day had started out being about numbers: I wanted to beat my group's score from the previous year, and I wanted to see how hard it would be to break 150. In the end, I realized it wasn't about numbers at all, but about seeing new birds, or seeing old birds in a new way, or finally being able to identify a bird by a diagnostic trait I hadn't recognized before. When I signed up for the birdathon, I expected the stress of a Kiwanis competition, where my skill would be scrutinized by an adjudicator. I still have a hard time driving past Langara Community College whenever I'm in Vancouver. I can still see myself walking onstage, desperate to please the competition judge and not quite measuring up. I was being asked to perform in a language that was not my own.

When the birdathon came to an end, we didn't submit our results to an arbiter. We knew exactly what we had seen—and the common birds we had dipped out on. In addition to our final tally, we also assembled a list of "how on earth did we not see that?" birds, which included such obvious species as mute swan, red-tailed hawk, and rock pigeon. We laughed when we got to the pigeon, because how often does it happen that one goes anywhere without seeing a pigeon?

And as for the competition itself? I realized that the word was a bit of a misnomer. In a birdathon, you're in it for the birds. We saw 131 species that day and missed the previous year's record by two, but I ended the day counting down the months to my next birdathon.

Zen Birder

WE NEVER SAW THE ELEGANT TROGON IN ARIZONA. IN SPITE of the fact that I'd hired a highly recommended local guide, we had excellent weather, we were in the bird's precise habitat and we'd even run into two border patrol officials on ATVs who claimed that the birds were "literally everywhere." That might have been a slight exaggeration, but the trogon had been seen in the canyon both on the morning we arrived and the day before, and was seen the day after as well.

That's the beauty and the frustration of birding. You can't count on anything being there when you want it to be. So often, birds have other plans.

That I managed to convince my husband to travel to southeastern Arizona, the epicentre of birding, still boggles my mind. I convinced him by showing him pictures of Chiricahua National Monument's hoodoos and precariously balancing rocks that looked majestic even by his erudite sci-fi/fantasy standards. Besides, he enjoys having trips planned for him, and there was the added lure of blue sky in December.

WE HAD COME BACK TO ARIZONA TO BIRD. FOUR YEARS PRIOR, in that very same state, I'd nearly thrown away my binoculars. Back then, I was a true novice birder. I confused a hummingbird with an exotic insect, and the only birds I saw clearly were two multicoloured Andean parrots hanging off our eccentric neighbour's T-shirt. My binocular skills were such that I really only saw a bird if it posed for me, the way a family of great-horned owls did, each sitting immovable on a branch, next door to our bed and breakfast's property. Like any self-respecting birder, the first thing I did was buy a field guide to the birds of Arizona; what I failed to do—because I didn't know how—was actually study the guide. Instead, I played the reverse guessing game. I flipped through the pages, decided on a few birds I was dying to see, and proceeded to imagine seeing them wherever I went.

By the third day, I had put away the book and stopped trying to identify anything whatsoever. But that same day, I nearly saw a red-faced warbler in Oak Creek Canyon. I wouldn't have known of the existence of a red-faced warbler, or his possible whereabouts, had I not met a couple of birders who were standing under a tree, craning their necks in a particularly self-satisfied manner.

"Have you seen anything exciting?" This seems to be code among birders for hi, how are you, what's in the neighbourhood, and in the event that you've seen something extraordinary that a beginner is unlikely to have noticed, could you please help me out? Or at least that's what I meant when I uttered the phrase.

"Just a red-faced warbler."

"Here?"

"Yes—up in these trees." The man in the multipocketed vest pointed upward, but all I could see were about twenty trees competing for a tiny piece of blue sky.

"Over there?" I pointed right.

"In that general direction."

And off they went—but not before showing me a picture of a red-faced warbler in their Sibley guide, and not before I decided that this was my all-time favourite bird because how often do you see a bird with a crimson face sporting a black headband? A minute before, I had been blissfully ignorant of the existence of red-faced warblers; it took one look at the picture to turn me into a maniacally, insatiably greedy hoarder of a birder. I wanted the warbler sighting and I wanted it immediately, as good a look as that couple had. And off I went, stumbling over tree roots, binoculars pointed upward, seeing nothing but "leaf birds," which are only slightly less frustrating than their cousins, the "just-flew birds" or the infamous "it'll-be-here-as-soon-as-you-leave birds." I caught a few backlit specimens, but had no idea what they were, and the couple that had seen the red-faced warbler had long since disappeared.

I had been spoiled in Toronto. As the only beginner in my small birding group, I received preferential treatment. Everybody made sure I saw whatever was out there. Nobody ever pointed to enormous pine trees and said, "Oh, it's somewhere there" and walked off before I too had enjoyed a good look.

Part of the problem of the moment—which reduced me to tears and made me contemplate removing my binoculars, leaving them on the Oak Creek Canyon trail and quitting birding once and for all—was the conversation I'd had with my husband mere minutes before the red-faced warbler debacle.

"Look at that woodpecker flying by," I said.

"How can you tell it's a woodpecker?"

"The undulating flight pattern."

"The what?"

"Look, when it flies, it's like it's riding a wave. Unmistakably woodpecker-like. I'm pretty sure that one was an acorn—they're common in Arizona."

It likely wasn't an acorn woodpecker. I had no idea how to identify the bird when it wasn't in my field guide, and I wouldn't have noticed its diagnostic white wing markings, which make it a very close relative of our red-headed woodpecker. But my tone in the moment oozed smugness. I didn't mean to rub it in that I knew more than Leon did about birds, but actually I did mean to, a little bit. I wanted him to be impressed with my knowledge. I wanted him to acknowledge that the time spent in the field wasn't for naught and that, slowly but surely, I was becoming an expert. That my husband cared not one iota for my ornithological expertise and that he only wanted me to find joy in the pursuit of birds didn't cross my mind; I was so used to collecting pats on the head and affirmation for my intelligence that I hadn't stopped to consider my audience.

That birding might be an antidote to smugness might have occurred to me in the moment had I not been in the midst of a full-blown hissy fit.

"If I can't even see a red-faced warbler, what's the point?"

"You'll see it another time."

"There won't be another time. I'm an inept birder. What's the point of another one of those?" I wailed, wiping my nose on my sleeve. Things degenerated from there, and by the time we reached the car I was already questioning the point of my very existence.

In my failure-induced stupor, I made it back to the car and was about to begin my meticulously prepared monologue, in which I would thank my husband for the binoculars he had bought me two years ago, but that, alas, the time had come to toss poor old Zeiss into a garbage bin, along with my new *Birds of Arizona* field guide because... and at that very moment, another acorn woodpecker—or what I took to be an acorn woodpecker—whizzed by me, practically demanding that I attend to its gorgeous physique and fixate my attention on the crimson cap adorning its head.

And without thinking, I obeyed. Instead of throwing away my binoculars in a fit of irrational rage (the prepared monologue had accompanying actions, too), I picked them up and followed the slick, tuxedoed acorn woodpecker as it swept across my line of vision, into the sky, into a tree, through the branches, behind the trunk, tap-tap-tap, over my head and back again.

I didn't quit birding. I didn't throw away my fantastic Zeiss binoculars, a feat of German optics that far exceeded my birding prowess and that let me see birds in Technicolor. I persevered through the frustration—and the unnerving reality that I would never be a first-rate birder.

FOUR YEARS LATER, WE RETURNED TO ARIZONA, AND THIS time I came with a different attitude. I may have erred in the other direction, because everything I saw brought me to paroxysms of joy, whether it was the Montezuma's quail that I accidentally flushed, the vermillion flycatcher that perched reliably on a post in the Patagonia-Sonoita

Creek Preserve, a lone black-throated grey warbler, which I identified with relative ease, or the four roadrunners that crisscrossed our path when we least expected to see them. By the time we met up with our bird guide, Matt Brown, a hardy transplant to southern Arizona from Upstate New York, my meagre wish list had already been exhausted, with the exception of the pygmy nuthatch—which I was curious about for its apparent lack of neck, but turned out to live in a completely different altitude zone. So we proceeded to the Peña Blanca Canyon, just north of Nogales, for its fine roster of warblers and the elusive elegant trogon, which had been seen that very morning.

On the way there, we picked up a cactus wren and a Bewick's wren, a verdin, and woodpeckers of many persuasions. We walked in the canyon searching for the elegant trogon and I noticed our guide getting anxious. It may have been a mistake to tell him about my red-faced warbler conniption four years ago. He was determined to get me a trogon at all costs.

"Let's just go a little farther, guys."

"Sure."

"I swear the bird was here this morning."

"It's not a problem. If we don't see it this time, we'll be back." My husband stared at me. Here I was, counselling our bird guide, assuring him that it didn't actually matter, that I was okay with things as they were, that the greatest pleasure, for me, was walking and happening upon whatever we saw.

Matt pished and walked into dense shrubs, trying desperately to get the birds for us. Leon had never seen anybody attract birds by imitating their calls with a series of vocalizations that sound like a nervous rendition of "pish, pish, psssssssh!" repeated ad nauseam, and he stared at me in disbelief. I nodded to him, as an acknowledgement that oh yes this is completely bonkers but it's what the professionals do and sometimes it even works.

The sun was starting to set, and I suggested turning back, but Matt must have feared my oncoming meltdown because he seemed unstoppable. When we finally gave up on the trogon, we noticed movement in a nearby tree and it turned out to be a painted redstart, one of the more stunning Arizona warblers, with its fiery red belly and black body. And right after the redstart, we got the bridled titmouse, which likely carries the award for cutest bird known to humankind, with its perky little crest and dainty bill. The titmouse looks a bit like the teenager who just got out of bed and forgot to tame his hair; a little on the shy side, looking slightly baffled by the world at large. I could relate to this bird.

No matter how hard we tried, the elegant trogon had other plans that day. As we packed up to go home, Matt said he hoped we weren't disappointed.

"All the more reason to come back," I said.

Who was this person talking? This person who suddenly didn't care that she'd come all the way to Arizona and missed such an obvious target bird? I had no idea who she was, but I kind of liked her.

My husband stared at me in disbelief, and Matt said, "You guys are such a joy to bird with. You just love whatever you see. What a breath of fresh air." Apparently, some people yell at him when he fails to locate their target birds.

And I wanted to tell him that this seemingly Zen birder before him, well, she wasn't born that way. She was a forty-something-year-old work-in-progress.

The More You See, the More You Want to See

SPRING BIRDING IS WHAT I LIVE FOR. AND YET MAY IS ALSO the month when I find myself the most anxious. As my friend Monika put it, "The bird FOMO is sometimes hard to take." Before the age of eBird, where I can see exactly who has seen which bird in which location, at what specific time, I think I was happier.

Here is what life looked like a mere two years ago: in May, I would go out birding, see as many warblers as I could and return home entirely fulfilled and glowing. Well, that's not exactly true. Two years ago, I would return home perplexed and wondering whether I had correctly ID'd the warblers I'd seen and a little concerned that I'd labelled everything that wasn't a show-stopping Blackburnian or Cape May warbler as a female common yellowthroat. To be brutally honest, two years ago, I couldn't ID much and that too put a damper on things.

Now, when I come home from birding, the first thing I do is check eBird to find out what else was seen in that particular location. eBird is a phenomenal resource: a large-scale citizen science project, it's a forum where birders post their lists worldwide. It has become an essential tool for conservation and bird monitoring. It's also a way of connecting with other birders and can be fantastically helpful when planning trips. I've only scratched the surface of the website's potential, but it has already tapped into my deepest anxiety and increased my FOMO—fear of missing out—exponentially. To know exactly what I missed, especially during the month of May—which seems to be about missing as much as it is about seeing, since one can't manage to be everywhere at once, especially when one lives on a migratory flyway—is devastating.

Last spring, after a trip out to Colonel Samuel Smith Park to find a reported least bittern, I came home to the most dreadful news: the least bittern I'd gone out to find had poked its head out of the reeds exactly five minutes after my departure.

Two years before, I might have thought, well, I gave the least bittern my best shot, I'll try again next year. Instead, I felt like a failure. Not only was it there, but I missed it by a matter of minutes. And that whimbrel I saw flying overhead? Well, had I stayed an hour longer, I would have seen a thousand whimbrels.

In 2018, eBird traffic exploded when a team of researchers from the Cornell Lab of Ornithology travelled to Tadoussac, Quebec, during spring migration. They were hoping to see a few thousand warblers, but what they saw exceeded all expectations and has gone down in birdwatching history as the single biggest day ever. They saw over 700,000 migratory birds. One of the observers reported that thousands of Tennessee, magnolia and myrtle warblers flew between his legs. Many of the birds were so close that one could count them without binoculars. I couldn't muster up true FOMO when I saw these numbers, because they defied all logic and expectation. Bird numbers on checklists that I frequent are usually measured in single or double digits, never in hundreds of thousands, and I cheered in disbelief: 72,220 Tennessee warblers, 50,500 American redstarts, 108,200 Cape May warblers and an equal number of magnolia warblers, 144,300 bay-breasted warblers, 28,900 Blackburnians and 14,400 Canada warblers, among the highlights.

"I have an idea for next year's vacation," I said to Leon.

"What bird did you find this time?"

"Tadoussac, Quebec. The skies have been darkening with warblers. It's almost like a passenger pigeon flight! They even saw 17,000 cedar waxwings."

"Have you been spending time on eBird again?"

"I'm telling you, Tadoussac is paradise in May."

"I thought you said that about Pelee."

"It's better. You wouldn't believe what they're seeing."

But Leon wasn't in the mood to be supportive of my latest eBird fantasies, since all spring he'd watched me shed tears over the birds I was missing.

THE DAY EBIRD TOLD ME THAT I'D MISSED THE LEAST BIT-tern, I took out my field guides and studied the bird. Two days later, I went back out to Colonel Samuel Smith Park and found the bird. I now knew more specifically where to look (and for how long) and did manage to get phenomenal looks at it. In the end, I wasn't the one who found the bird; after searching for an hour, I left to find some whimbrels, and on returning found two other gentlemen there who had their eyes on it. I later ran into some acquaintances and repaid the favour by showing them the bittern, and you should have seen the looks on their faces: the exact same intense gratitude and awe that I had just bestowed upon the folks who had helped me find the bird.

Each May, I see a lot—and miss out on just as much, if not more. One of the greatest hazards of falling in love with birds is that it revolves around the pursuit of something. The more you see, the more you want to see. And where there is pursuit, there lies endless disappointment, because it seems you'll never get there quickly enough and you'll never see quite enough.

But in the end, I'd rather have some FOMO than miss spring birding. Because there's endless appreciation for the things you do see, too, and with that comes the most profound joy.

The Little Bee-Eater and
the Steppe Buzzard

IT WASN'T MY DECISION TO VISIT GAN GAROO, ISRAEL'S ONLY
Australian park, with koalas and kangaroos milling about,
near the kibbutz where we stayed on the outskirts of Beit
She'an. I had wanted to visit the ruins of a Byzantine town
once called Scythopolis, but Leon's soft spot for petting
zoos prevailed, much to the surprise of our cousins, who
warned us that the park was geared toward the ten-year-
old set.

"I've always wanted to see koalas," Leon said.

"Didn't we see them at the zoo in Toronto?"

"I'd like to see them in Israel."

I decided that two hours in Gan Garoo was worth the
compromise, since it would give me leverage when negoti-
ating a longer birding excursion and an additional trip to
the banding station in Eilat.

We ended up being the first to arrive at Gan Garoo, and
until 10:00 a.m., we were the only ones there. We did what
everyone does in an Australian petting zoo that happens

to be in Israel: we offered bits of apple to the parrots, and I dutifully took photos of Leon in front of a galloping kangaroo. He enjoyed himself and wanted to take photos of every animal, including all the Australian waterfowl.

"Why are you taking so many photos?"

"You can check them in the field guide later."

"But I'm not interested in Australian waterfowl. I've barely mastered eastern North American ducks."

"In case we go to Australia. At least you'll know their ducks."

Leon's programming mind focuses on optimization at every turn. My knowledge and interest in Australian birds was limited to kookaburras, and I hadn't really planned on mastering Australian waterfowl while in Israel.

And just as he mentioned the ducks, the children started arriving. Families with four, five, six children appeared, strollers began multiplying and I had the impression that adults in the park searched for our children rather than making eye contact with us. Once they realized we had come alone, to feed the koalas *ourselves*, they stared, uncomfortable. Amidst the chaos of boisterous children, I instantly felt a lack of something significant in my own life. I felt like I was branded with a sign that highlighted my childlessness. This was a place *for* children.

I remembered a passage in *Anna Karenina* where Dolly, Anna's sister-in-law and the quintessential Tolstoyan mother, who prides herself on her maternal qualities, visits Vronsky's estate and is horrified to see the place childless and the adults play-acting as if they were children. She found the spectacle unnatural. Though nobody talked to me, I felt everybody was looking at me through Dolly's eyes, and I suddenly felt that there was something unnatural about the way I lived my life, the decision to accept child-lessness and not fight harder to remedy the situation—and here we were, at Gan Garoo, my husband and me, both playing at being children.

And then, out of nowhere, a goat ran up to me and ripped a paper map out of my hand and devoured it, right under the sign that said, "Do NOT feed the goats any-thing but goat food. It may poison them." Not only was I possibly unfit to have children, but I had likely given a goat indigestion.

Just as I tried to recover from the goat incident, which sent me running out of the pen as quickly as I could, I came face to face with the largest, most flamboyant white peacock I've ever seen. He calmly pranced toward me, tail feathers spread in a semicircular pattern, and then turned away and walked toward his lady friend, whom he clearly had to impress because he started half-strutting, half-dancing toward her, doing everything in his power to merit her attention.

I watched, still clutching the remnants of my map of Gan Garoo, marvelling at the way nature just takes over for most creatures. Natural selection. So much of bird life and behaviour—from the bright colours, to the hypnotic or downright peculiar mating displays, to the songs—revolves around their need to procreate, to demonstrate the fitness of their genes.

Somehow, I had fallen out of step with the biological imperative. Here in Gan Garoo, I felt more on display than the most exotic peacock, who returned, once he had seduced his lady friend and knew she'd be waiting to partake of his services later. He came back and ambled around us nonchalantly, his very presence bordering on the ridiculous, and for the first time I laughed at the goat, at our trip to Gan Garoo, at the fact that for an hour I had believed that people were looking at me and questioning my life choices, when really all the adults were trying to do was to make sure their children didn't put their hands in an animal's mouth by accident.

Still, I wore my sunglasses inside all afternoon.

BIRDS SAVED ME IN ISRAEL. NOT THE PEACOCK OR THE PARrots or the Australian waterfowl that I never bothered to ID; not the hoopoe that I saw wandering about the streets of Tel Aviv, with a regal strut, flaunting his radiant crest; not the imposing pelicans that flew low over our kibbutz every morning. We spent our last days in Israel on the shore of the Red Sea, in Eilat, mostly out of nostalgia; my husband had been there twenty years earlier and had fond memories of seeing multicoloured tropical fish in the sea. He wanted me to experience those same fish, even though he knew full well that although I'm an enthusiastic swimming-pool swimmer, I almost never submerge my head when swimming in open water. I'm petrified of what lies beneath.

I found a bird guide to take us around Eilat. I tried, unsuccessfully, to hide my amazement when our guide, Itai Shanni, turned out to be one of the judges for the Champions of the Flyway birding competition. I was starstruck. We began the day at a raptor count in the mountains above Eilat, where elite birders worked in shifts, clicker in hand, in an effort to count every single bird flying overhead. The counters had tallied 6,000 raptors by the time we arrived; apparently, a big day there yields 250,000 raptors. I watched the raptors, mesmerized by the sight, but I couldn't tell a steppe buzzard from a black kite from a hobby from a Levant sparrowhawk from a honey buzzard. I hadn't done my raptor homework before coming to Israel. Leon was in heaven. He appreciates these fierce, manly birds, as he calls them, and can watch them soar for hours. I, on the other hand, am partial to the diminutive side of the spectrum, the little multicoloured birds. It wasn't until we descended the mountain and found ourselves birding around a lagoon that I saw my first little green bee-eater perched on a wire, and I knew exactly what I had come for. A slender bird with a bronzed green head and a robust turquoise neck, and with elongated central tail feathers topping off the ensemble—I'd never seen anything like it. I'd like to credit the resplendent bird for letting me forget about Gan Garoo, the map-devouring goat and all the children I would never have, but really it was the act of looking itself, of immersing myself in the intricacies of this fantastical, Technicolor plumage, and trying to commit every nuance of the moment to memory, that made me look past myself for a while.

I OFTEN FORGET THE SIZE DIFFERENTIAL BETWEEN MY HUSband and me, and it's only when I look at photos that I pause, and sometimes laugh. We're the most unlikely pair: a six-foot-one powerlifter with a collection of kettle bells (many of which outweigh me), and a five-foot-two writer/adult-ballet-aficionado. I doubt any algorithm on eHarmony would have suggested we contact one another. Neither one of us would have swiped right on Tinder, especially since his photo on dating sites featured him emerging from the waters of Lake Simcoe wearing a fetching Speedo, while I appeared in my Comparative Literature PhD uniform: a black leather jacket, dark-rimmed glasses and a scarf tied through a loop, the way a friend had taught me in Rome. He was too buff, I was too nerdy. It's a good thing Internet dating had failed both of us—otherwise we might never have resorted to more archaic means.

It dawned on me how different we are when I marvelled at the emerald colouring of the little green bee-eater, with electric blue plumage on either side of the black mask that sets off his crimson eyes. My husband took one look at this paragon of elegance and turned away, once again raising his binoculars toward the sky, hoping for another kettle of buzzards. He'd had enough of tiny multicoloured birds: he craved something fiercer, more powerful, more primal.

I felt a little bad for our tour guide, who didn't know whom to placate in this situation; I was clearly the more enthusiastic birder, and I demanded colourful, dashing creatures, but my husband was the one with bulging back muscles and biceps almost as big as our guide's head.

From the outside, that's exactly what we look like, the two of us: a little green bee-eater and a steppe buzzard. To imagine that there exists a world that holds both of these wildly different creatures within its realm, to imagine that they somehow coexist within the same geographic range— dare I say happily—to imagine such an incongruous pairing of the most unlikely species, feels nothing short of magic.

Snowy Owl

I NEVER TIRE OF SNOWY OWLS, THE MOST REGAL OF RAPTORS and the sight I look forward to every winter. I never had to chase a snowy owl, because before I saw my first one, I didn't know they existed.

Brete organized a weekday outing to Whitby on New Year's Eve in 2011 to chase the smew, a duck that had absolutely no business being in southern Ontario, since it breeds in subarctic Siberia and winters in Germany and occasionally the UK; its usual North American appearances rarely extend beyond Alaska. In fact, the sighting was so rare that every self-respecting twitcher—the sort of birder who chases birds obsessively—suddenly appeared to be hunting for motels in the eastern suburbs of Toronto. Even legendary competitive birder John Vanderpoel flew to Toronto from Virginia, madly hoping to add one more bird to his Big Year list before the new year. In the end, he finished his 2011 Big Year competition in first place, with 744 birds, but missed the smew by two days.

And so did we. But the non-sighting didn't disappoint me, largely because I had no idea the bird existed; it's such a rare occurrence in eastern North America that it wasn't even listed in my field guide. A cross between a merganser and a bufflehead, with a bit of a common goldeneye personality, the smew would have to wait until I could head over to Europe to catch a glimpse of it. As we bade farewell to Whitby harbour, a fellow birder wished us a "Happy Smew Year," which I found equal parts cute and disturbing. (I've taken to using it regularly.)

But before we left, Brete insisted that we walk a little farther, toward the pier, even though some of us could barely stand upright on account of the wind. To minimize the walking, he set up his scope and scanned the length of the pier, including the half-dozen lamp posts.

"Oh, I see it!"

"A smew?"

"Not unless it looks like a big white owl."

I ran up to the scope and couldn't believe it. A sleek, white bird with yolk-coloured eyes and a sharp, diamond-shaped bill built to hunt rodents—but that really could pierce anything, including another of its own species. I watched the snowy owl open and close its eyes a couple of times and rotate its neck nearly 280 degrees. A few years later, I would think of the snowy owl every time I did a spotting exercise in ballet class, longing for the built-in biological advantage of being able to whip my head around without altering the posture of my body.

We watched the owl until our feet became numb, but even then we didn't want to leave. Part of me was grateful that this bird was a complete surprise to me, and yet another part burned slightly, knowing that I'd never again have the experience of seeing a snowy owl for the first time. A few years later, when I saw my first great grey owl in the small hamlet of Brooklin, Ontario, I watched a woman break down in tears of joy at the sight of her first great grey. I'll admit that I let out a squeal that was probably audible to all fifty birders standing at the edge of the road, but this woman has having a St.-Teresa-of-Avila moment of ecstasy, replete with moans, sighs and unabashed weeping. An emotional business this was, birding.

The snowy owl sighting meant that all I wanted thereafter was more snowy owls. It's still the highlight of my winter. I've seen them on the ice, standing on a rubble pile at Tommy Thompson Park, in the middle of a snowy field, on lamp posts and hydro wires, and even once lounging on a branch atop a pine tree, as if it were an ottoman. Snowies are not rare in the Toronto area—with a little luck, and some perusing of the local birding listservs, it's really quite hard to miss them.

TWO FRIENDS FROM THE BANDING STATION, BOTH ADEPT AT snowy owl banding, invited me to go road trapping with them in late February 2016. We piled into Bronwyn's old Toyota Camry and the day started out slowly, with the requisite hour-long traffic jam on the way out of Toronto, but once we were on the back roads about an hour north of the city, we were alone with the elements. And the owls. I stared out the window, surveying fields and hydro poles, looking for large whitish blobs everywhere. I sat in the back with the traps and the faint stench of hamsters and mice, which ended up smelling like fine perfume by the end of the day, so altered was my state of mind. I had once managed six snowy owls in one day and had considered that the apex of good fortune. This day's count of twelve would leave me speechless.

The entire time that we drove the snow-dusted back roads, I was singularly occupied by the task of observing my surroundings. If someone had told me, even a year before, that I would be able to sit still for eight hours and simply look out the window for white blobs against a mostly white background, and that I could do this without pulling my hair out and dying of boredom, I would have laughed out loud.

I HAD SPENT MOST OF THAT WINTER WISHING I WERE ELSEwhere, dreaming of some other elusive place. It's a frustrating place to inhabit, this wanting something other. It had started a few months earlier, with the birth of my nephew, whom I realized I loved even before I met him. Watching him slowly gain weight, learn to focus his gaze, smile, grip a finger. Those first months of his life, I found myself writing him letters constantly, both in my mind and in reality. Letters I never sent, in response to questions he hadn't asked, but which I imagined he might, one day. How would I explain my life to him? How would I tell him that instead of a baby, I have a poster with 750 birds of North America, and that sometimes, walking by avian families on my way to the bathroom, I feel something like kinship? How would I tell him about our half-hearted attempts at the fertility clinic, where we tried several different procedures, even though the doctor had pointed out the low statistical chances and tapped her manicured fingernail on the single-digit percentage on the printout? FSH levels, LH surge and AMH hormones became household words; we dispensed fertility shorthand with smug nonchalance and joked about Leon's slothful sperm that seemed to be in no hurry whatsoever to attack my eggs, but neither of us could commit to the next barrage of more invasive procedures.

I wrote my nephew long tracts, self-justifications, explanations. I wanted so badly to convey that somehow my life did have purpose, that what I was doing wasn't at all what I thought I'd be doing, but that in spite of it all, I was inching toward happiness.

And yet the whole time I was writing to him, I wanted to be somewhere else. I fantasized about moving, about life after Leon's retirement, when we could escape our mundane Toronto life and trade in traffic for southern Arizona or Reykjavik. After a few hours spent Googling properties and determining that neither place offered Yiddish or adult ballet classes, I suddenly remembered my nephew, Augie, whose sweet, wide-eyed baby face had already imprinted itself on my heart, and I felt guilty that I was thinking of disappearing from his life before I'd even gotten to know him. That thought alone made me seek solace in chasing birds, because the one calming thing about being in their presence is the knowledge that my existence, to them, is entirely immaterial. The last thing birds care about is self-justification; they don't even notice me.

AND THEN, IN BRONWYN'S CAMRY, FOR THE FIRST TIME THAT winter, I found myself happy exactly where I was, looking intently for white on white, eyes growing feeble in the midday light. Birding is a master class in learning how to see and how to be present.

The banding was slow. We put out the trap several times, but the owls either flew off or ignored it altogether. Bronwyn and Charlotte kept asking me if I was okay, if I wasn't disappointed, and I kept telling them that the act of looking gave me the greatest pleasure of all.

After lunch, we set up a hamster trap for a gorgeous male who was eyeing us from a hydro pole, but he absconded in a different direction. We were about to move the trap, when an enormous female appeared out of nowhere and swooped down toward the poor little rodent. Charlotte extracted the owl from the trap masterfully—in a matter of seconds—and suddenly there we were in the car with a two-and-a-half-kilogram snowy owl. I didn't hold her, but I kept petting her head and mumbling absurdities about how she was the cutest thing in the world after my baby nephew. I took off my coat, oblivious to the cold in the rush of adrenaline and the realization that in a matter of minutes this would all turn into a surreal memory. And then, after she was banded, we stood outside, measuring her wing, weighing her (2,515 grams!), photographing her; I could feel my fingers slowly growing numb, and I wondered what I was doing outside in just a hoodie with no coat, and then before I knew it I saw Bronwyn turn away from us, shift her weight to her left foot, her right leg lifted slightly, her arms thrown upward—through a third arabesque line—almost lifting off herself as she released the owl. The owl flapped her majestic wings and flew away from us, deep into the field, past our sightline.

THAT DAY IN THE CAR, WE TALKED ABOUT EVERYTHING FROM Bronwyn's education to her plans for after she received her MA, to her thesis, her family, her brother, marriage, dreams, goals. But mostly we talked about birds and how much we loved them. When she wasn't extracting birds from mist nets or studying birds or teaching field biology classes, she was getting to know every single common grackle in her neighbourhood. She had a photo album full of identical-looking grackles, but she could talk about the behaviour and feeding habits and individual traits of each specimen for hours. How a person could find such depth and meaning in a largish, blackish backyard bird I could not fathom.

She asked about my nephew, and we talked about family, about food, her peanut allergy, her plans to stay in her parents' house after they passed and take care of her brother. She mentioned the fanfiction she wrote about Richard III and lamented no longer having the time to learn Japanese. And then we were back to birds, her research on migratory stopover points, her excitement about opening the banding station for the season, the grackles. We compared notes on our favourite warblers and she remembered every bird I had extracted at the station.

IN MY MEMORY, THE ROAD CONDITIONS THAT DAY WERE TERrible. Bronwyn's car didn't have snow tires, and when we skidded a few times, I remember being thankful that I wasn't the one driving and just hoping for a safe trip home. We saw a dozen snowies, some pure white males, but mostly fierce, grey-speckled females, whom everybody feared, rodents and male owls alike. Female snowies are so strong that they can easily take down a male of their own species. Without thinking twice.

Nothing that day could have foretold that six weeks later, Bronwyn would be driving down the same roads on a clear, sunny, bucolic Easter Sunday, and would come in contact with a minivan and be pronounced dead at the scene. At the moment of the accident, I was standing in front of the High Park reservoir, pointing out a wood duck to a friend, and commenting on its unreal beauty, as if someone had hand-painted it.

THERE WAS SOMETHING ABSURD ABOUT THAT SNOWY OWL day.

What I didn't know at the moment Charlotte was untangling the owl's legs from the trap was that we had an audience. Out of nowhere, a pickup truck had pulled up next to us, with two uniformed Ministry of Natural Resources employees. They watched the whole extraction spectacle before getting out of the car.

"What are you guys doing out here?"

"Banding raptors. We are with the Simcoe County Banding Group," Charlotte said. "I have my permit."

As he walked over to check her permit, which Charlotte retrieved from the back seat after handing over the beast of a bird to Bronwyn, he couldn't take his eyes off the owl. Instead of properly reading the permit, he took out his iPhone and I half-expected him to take a selfie with the bird, but he contented himself with closeups of the snowy, which he'd never seen in the hand before. All my photos from that day were photobombed by a Ministry of Natural Resources employee in a sharp-looking, fur-trimmed hat and shades, staring at the enormous bird with rapture and disbelief.

We saw more owls that day than I'd seen in my lifetime, combined. We wanted so badly to catch another owl that we drove along the roads until we could no longer see the utility poles. We wanted so badly for the day not to end. If I had known that it would be the last time I saw Bronwyn,

I would have memorized every word of our exchange; I would have come home and written it down.

In the months that followed Bronwyn's death, I kept returning to that day. Maybe we had been too happy, maybe we had tempted fate somehow by driving on those icy roads. Maybe the accident was somehow payback for the perfect day we'd never asked for, the perfect day we had.

I think of Bronwyn every week when I volunteer at the banding station. Her walking stick still stands by the door. I imagine there's a benevolent ghost watching over me as I fumble through bird extractions. And when I close my eyes, I can still see her long fingernails deftly manoeuvring the nets, with such swiftness and grace that the bird emerges from a tangle of netting in a matter of seconds. Wordlessly, fingers working with a precision I never imagined possible.

A few years later, I scribed while a friend was banding a common grackle. The bird was furious at being constrained, flapping its wings violently and letting out a series of frustrated guttural squeaks, but amidst the fidgeting, I had the chance to inspect its yellow eye and its magically iridescent bluish head, which glistened in the light. Remembering Bronwyn, I leaned over to pet its head. And as soon as I had my hand on the nape of its neck, the grackle swung around and I felt its sharp bill lacerate the side of my thumb.

IT'S BEEN A FEW YEARS NOW SINCE BRONWYN'S DEATH, since those letters I wrote right after my nephew's birth, and the two events now feel intertwined in my mind. The line between life and death in the bird world is often invisible. We tend to romanticize birds—these cute, dainty things— but they can be ruthless. When a snowy owl hunts, she'll maul a rodent to death with vigour. I once saw a snowy owl dismembering a duck (perhaps a white-winged scoter?), diving into it and devouring it with gusto. The northern shrike's nickname—butcher bird—felt entirely abstract until I came upon one methodically impaling a vole on a thorn and proceeding to disembowel the tiny rodent before my eyes. I've never been a lover of voles, but I did feel for this particular creature, which had likely done no wrong, apart from existing, on this particular day. And yet for birds, it's not a matter of cruelty, it's a question of survival. And where there is life, there is also, often simultaneously, a vicious, uncalled-for death. I'm reminded that nature is as cruel as it is magnificent.

But where the natural world always manages to strike a balance, whereas one can explain how species predation and death serve larger ecological goals, Bronwyn's senseless death defied any of that. There wasn't a larger ecosystem at stake. There was a young woman, in her car, on the cusp of a promising ornithological career, a woman whose fierce love of birds had taken her to James Bay and South Africa, and brought her to the banding station an hour before sunrise, six days a week, and in winter transported her to deserted country roads north of Toronto, hunting for raptors.

And then there wasn't.

THE LAST PHOTO I HAVE OF BRONWYN DALZIEL IS A DISEM-bodied image of her hands, bright pink from the cold, holding the owl. Her long fingernails are unmistakable. There she stands, clutching the owl's legs just above the talons in her left hand, gripping the enormous bird firmly against her body, her right hand resting against its wing. I return to the photograph from time to time and wish I hadn't framed it around the owl's body. Because what I no longer have tangible proof of is the completely satisfied smile on Bronwyn's face. That she held the owl with joy, in spite of the freezing temperatures, in spite of the bird's claws, so close to her skin.

What's Your Favourite Bird?

"WHAT'S YOUR FAVOURITE BIRD?" I HATE THIS QUESTION AND yet I ask it of everybody I know. My own list shifts constantly—it depends on the season, and it changes to accommodate rarities and my current nemesis bird. I'm also loyal to my first sightings, and those still top my list when contemplating favourites.

But if I could get a bird inked on my body, it would be the American woodcock, the largest North American shorebird, which hangs out mostly on damp ground in the woods, perfectly camouflaged with its surroundings. To me, the bird looks like an accident of nature, its eyes grotesquely close together, perched high up on its head, giving it almost 360 degrees of vision for detecting predators, and a long, ultra-sensitive bill for probing the ground for worms that it cannot see. Stocky, short-legged, incessantly pouting, this is a bird with attitude. And yet the American woodcock is also one of the more curious Don Juans of the avian world; in early spring, at dusk, the bird engages in an aerial mating dance that counts among the more peculiar things I've ever seen.

The aerial display of the woodcock is so odd that many birding clubs host outings just to bear witness to the bird's eccentric pre-mating performance. It begins with a nasal *peent*, repeated more times than strictly necessary. Ornithology oracle Frank Chapman calls that *peent* "the first notes of his love song." And if a nasal note weren't enough to get a girl going, what follows is nothing short of spectacular. The pouty, stocky woodcock hurls himself high into the ether "on whistling wings," ascending in a series of wide circles, as if he'd suddenly developed the agility of a nymph. Then he plummets to the ground with a yelp—and does the acrobatic feat all over again. These *peents* and aerial dances work like a charm in the spring; the American woodcock mates morning and night without fail for eight straight weeks. What female wouldn't be seduced by such a show? After witnessing the stocky bird's transformation into an aerial gymnast, even I could be convinced to mate with a woodcock.

But transformative magic aside, I relish the woodcock's demeanour: he's so very much his own bird.

IF I COULD GIVE AN AWARD TO MY FAVOURITE, BEST-DRESSED bird, it would be the northern flicker, in honour of the cacophonic plumage he flaunts. Who ever said that polka-dots and dark stripes and red blots and flashy yellow wing and tail feathers and a jet-black handlebar mustache don't all belong on the same bird?

Until I started birding in earnest and met the flicker, I remember walking into clothing shops crippled with anxiety, staring at sweaters without a clue as to what suited me. I remember approaching salespeople in desperation, hoping they would tell me what to buy, what would look good on me. My mother and sister both knew how to dress, but every time I put an outfit together, it didn't look quite right. Something was off. I tried shopping with both my mom and my sister and ended up coming home with clothes that I wouldn't wear. The colours weren't bright enough, and the waistlines were too high, the shoes uncomfortable, the shoulders too broad. I couldn't even pinpoint what was wrong; it just didn't feel like me.

The day I saw the northern flicker sporting his busy attire with perfect confidence, I decided that if he could do it, I could too. I had always tried to buy clothes that made me look like everyone else; what would happen if I just bought things that made me smile?

I also fell for the northern flicker when I learned that Roger Tory Peterson, the most famous twentieth-century birder, the one who popularized the modern, portable field guide, counted it as his favourite bird. If Peterson registered the sublime in this regular North American breeder, then I could too. The fact that loving the northern flicker put me in Peterson's illustrious company, however tangentially, made me love him all the more.

IT'S IMPOSSIBLE TO ANSWER THE "FAVOURITE BIRD" QUEStion without mentioning warblers. These tiny neotropical migrants, which arrive in late April from their South or Central American wintering grounds, putter around for a month and head north to breed intensely, then perform the whole migratory ritual again, southbound, year after year, no matter the weather, are nothing short of extraordinary. Emblems of spectacular, intrepid tenacity, I couldn't imagine my life without devoting the month of May to their pursuit.

But a favourite warbler? I've now seen some visually stunning ones, including the Cape May, the Blackburnian, the painted redstart, the Prothonotary, whose yellow has a twist of orange—he's the Meyer lemon of warblers—and the Canada warbler, whose necklace I'd like to copy and wear. I've had arguments with friends at the banding station about the value of subtlety; there are those who wax lyrical about the female black-throated blue, and while I'm thrilled to no longer misidentify her, the white handkerchief on a mostly olive-coloured body doesn't quite make my heart race.

If we're talking favourites, though, I'd have to turn back the clock to the first time I correctly identified a warbler on my own, and the champion there is indisputably the black-and-white warbler. Not only was it the first warbler I found myself, but it also stunned me with its elegant simplicity, and, on closer observation, its resemblance to a zebra trapped in a tiny songbird's body. Could anything top that?

THE TRUTH IS, I HAVE MANY FAVOURITE BIRDS. SO WHY DO I torment people with a question that I can't even answer myself? Because it opens the door to conversations about my very favourite thing: birds. And before we know it, we're trading photos of rarities and the commonest of birds, entering into friendly competition about what we've managed to see, learning about phenomenally strange avian behaviours.

My favourite bird changes depending on the family, the season, the rarity factor, whether I managed to locate the bird myself, whether we locked eyes in the field or not. But in general, unless I'm staring at gulls, or muttering obscenities under my breath while trying to distinguish a Baird's from a white-rumped sandpiper, my favourite bird is the one right in front of me.

Headache

WHEN PEOPLE LEARN THAT I GREW UP IN A HOUSE WITH FIVE pianos, they immediately assume I have a musical ear. Sure, I hummed along to Bartok's Sonata for Two Pianos before I could read, and I told friends that my favourite piece of music was a Liszt Mephisto Waltz, long before I had any idea who Mephistopheles really was.

"Birdsong will be a no problem for you," Brete assured me when I first started birding.

What they didn't know was that I had already tried and failed at musical dictation and ear training. Every Thursday, as a child, I used to go to solfège classes, where Mrs. Burashko would teach us mnemonics for recognizing musical intervals, among other things. The class was supposed to help me acquire pitch and eventually learn to sight-sing, but I never made it past the interval quizzes. I was a so-so piano student, but also the daughter of professional musicians who made sure they did everything in their power to prepare me for my annual music exams. The entire ear-training portion of the exam brought me nothing but anxiety, and all the notes seemed interchangeable to me.

I memorized the mnemonics. I knew that the first interval in "My Bonnie Lies over the Ocean" was a major sixth, and in the theme to *Love Story* it was a minor sixth. I knew that in "Twinkle, Twinkle" it was a perfect fifth, but the problem was that sometimes I sang "Twinkle, Twinkle" to "My Bonnie Lies over the Ocean" and there seemed to be very little that Mrs. Burashko could do beyond shake her head and wonder aloud in despair, "No! How can this be?"

WHEN I STARTED USING A BIRDSONG QUIZ APP CALLED Larkwire, I soon found I was as helpless as I had been in Mrs. Burashko's basement studio in the early 1990s. I was trying my hand at bird mnemonics, like "drink-your-tea" for the eastern towhee, "sweet-sweet-you're-so-sweet" for the yellow warbler, or "pleased-to-pleased-to-pleased-to-meet-cha" for the chestnut-sided warbler, and though it helped in the moment, I continued to hear most birds singing "drink-your-tea." After a while I conceded that this was going nowhere because I am tone-deaf. And also because when I'm out in the field, it's a rare occasion for me to hear songs in isolation. The tremendous challenge of birding by ear is that you have to pick out individual songs within a cacophonous mess, or, as my friend Jody Allair said, more pedagogically, while taking Leon and me on a bird walk, "It's like picking out instrument lines within a symphony."

The music of birds gave me a headache.

IN AN ESSAY CALLED "MOTHER AND MUSIC," MARINA Tsvetaeva writes about how her mother—a concert pianist—had done everything possible to encourage little Marina to follow in her footsteps, but it wasn't meant to be. Even as a child, she sat in front of her mother's musical score, which happened to be a piece for soprano and piano, and found herself drawn to the poetry of the words written out above the singer's line of music, each syllable set off with dashes. Already, though she couldn't yet properly read, she inhabited a different kind of word-based music. There was no way she could avoid disappointing her mother.

I first read Tsvetaeva in graduate school. I read and reread the essay and kept seeing myself in her words, imagining that I too had found a different kind of music, that mine too was word-based.

But there was yet another kind of music waiting for me: the music of a birdsong accompanied by finding a bird in the field and seeing it through my binoculars. Now *that* was the music I had been searching for. The slow process of getting to know a blue jay and all of its song variations, hearing it as I walk through my neighbourhood, noticing it where I wouldn't have known it existed before—that is the composite shape of music.

THE SONG OF THE EASTERN TOWHEE, THE "DRINK-YOUR-TEA" that everybody picks out with ease, brings me straight back to Mrs. Burashko's basement studio, where no matter how hard I studied my interval mnemonics, they became interchangeable when played in succession. Indeed, the eastern towhee did drink his tea when I listened to him on a CD in my car; he drank cups of Earl Grey, and I sang along to his tea-drinking with a hint of smugness. They're right! It really isn't that hard.

But when the eastern towhee sang in the field, surrounded by other riotous birds, it turned out that I couldn't discern his voice from that of a song sparrow or a robin or, embarrassingly, a common grackle. Suddenly everybody was shouting "drink-your-tea" in various pitches, modulations and rhythms. Nothing sounded the way it was supposed to.

THIS CACOPHONY TRANSPORTED ME BACK TO MY MUSICAL education. I had the required genes, but they must have been wrongly arranged. With a great deal of effort and practice and a bit of luck, I passed the last of my piano exams with a required ear-training component. The day I learned I had passed, I threw away all my ear-training materials and my "foolproof" mnemonic cards that turned out to be not at all foolproof. My pyrophobia was the only thing that stood between me and a ceremonial burning party.

I thought I had seen the last of my ear training. But now it has come back to haunt me. I still tackle birdsong quizzes regularly, with very little success.

The first season I volunteered at the banding station, I accompanied a bespectacled, soft-spoken man named Tom on a census walk, where we stopped at designated points on a set path and counted every species seen and heard. A weekday data entry employee, and a self-proclaimed weekend birdbrain, Tom had been doing the same weekly census count for ten years when I first met him, yet it was the part of the week he lived for. Tom's mastery of birdsong rivals the command for Latin case endings I once had in high school, when I read Virgil and dreamt of a career in classics. It goes beyond the basic mnemonics; he can discern dialects, and his speech quickens at the mere mention of regional peculiarities of chickadee songs in Alberta. He hears trills, picking out raspy tinges and hushed tones and playful innuendos where I can barely catch a sound, let alone puzzle through its qualities. Everywhere we went, he kept saying, "Yellow warbler," and though I knew they nested near the banding station in large numbers, I had no idea how he heard them. I had tried to learn the mnemonic "sweet-sweet-you're-so-sweet" but never detected it in the field.

"I can't hear any yellow warblers."

"They're everywhere!"

"But they're not singing the 'sweet-you're-so-sweet' song."

"Try listening for rhythm. It's a two-part song." And then I heard it: three longish beats, a caesura, followed by four staccato beats.

"Is it this one? Duh-duh-duh, da-da-da-da?"

"Yes. Exactly." I fully expected Tom to mock my pitchless rendition of the yellow warbler song, but he didn't. "Sometimes those mnemonics lead you astray. Focus on the rhythms instead."

And slowly I began to add the warbling vireo to my collection. "It warbles," Bronwyn once told me, and indeed, I could hear it hovering somewhat monotonously around a three-part tune, slightly reminiscent of my attempts to learn Czerny studies on the piano, where my right and left hand alternated weaving in and out of chromatic scales while whichever hand was free kept the beat with pronounced, staccato chords.

Once I learned the American robin's song, I started to understand the idea of a rose-breasted grosbeak as a "robin on speed" or a scarlet tanager as a "robin who sings with a very sore throat." And I finally developed a better grasp of the red-eyed vireo, who sounds like a more monotonous robin singing an endless loop; whereas the robin pauses, the red-eyed vireo doesn't even need to stop for breath. I sometimes think of him as a relentless robin.

Every spring, I internalize a few new songs.

I still tend to mishear most things when I'm out in the field. And often I hear what I want to hear rather than what the bird is singing. In early spring, it seems that every song out there is a black-and-white warbler's squeaky wagon-wheel song, largely because I want it to be.

WHEN I FIRST MET MY HUSBAND, THAT WAS HOW I approached our conversations.

I've always been an epistolophiliac—in every relationship, I relied on e-mails to clarify my position, to hash things out, to apologize retrospectively. The reliance on written apologies after the fact meant that I didn't ever have to be in the moment and listen and connect with someone right then and there. I'd always fallen in love with people based on their written expression, the depth of their e-mails. I read into every word.

The first thing that shocked me about my husband was that he refused to communicate via e-mail. And yet I persisted in my ways. I sent him daily e-mails, dissecting our every conversation, and following up on arguments with long, drawn-out analyses, filling him in on the genealogy of my actions. My e-mails offered him all the tools I believed he needed to fully understand me: family history, relationship baggage, fears, insecurities. As a last resort, I accepted that his lack of e-mails could be the result of a simple linguistic issue: English wasn't his first language. And so, I barraged him with e-mails in Russian.

Thankfully, he knew better than to read them. "I don't need longwinded e-mails to tell me who you are," he said.

"But I want to give you insight into the laboratory of my mind," I wailed.

"What does that even mean?"

Since then, I have learned to identify certain birds based on their "jizz," a peculiar abbreviation in the birding world for "general impression of sight and sound." I can quickly assess a bird and then, based on the glimpse I get of its behaviour and general appearance, hazard an educated guess as to its identity. The details are often fuzzy, but I can almost always place the bird within its family based on posture, flight pattern or general appearance.

Now, whenever Leon and I argue, I think of the black-and-white warbler, which I can recognize creeping headfirst down a tree trunk before I've even seen its distinctive zebra pattern. I remind myself not to read into every single detail as if it held oracular significance. Birds have taught me when to listen, when to pay close attention to detail, and when to just relinquish control and let the big picture carry me where I need to go.

MY MNEMONICS HAVEN'T GOTTEN THAT MUCH BETTER, BUT my ability to listen for other things, things I might recognize, has improved. I'm still tremendously challenged by birdsong, and I know that it will never become second nature to me, but that no longer scares me. I'm heartened by the fact that every year, I'll be able to detect a few more birds by sound. When I walk through my neighbourhood at dawn now, I can identify the American goldfinches muttering, American robins singing, northern cardinals feeling frisky or moderately annoyed, house finches chattering, house sparrows drumming, nuthatches nasally proclaiming their territory, and the odd downy woodpecker ending each phrase with a descending scale.

I may not yet be able to pinpoint the song of the eastern towhee when he's among friends and relatives, but I'm inching my way closer.

My Wild Side

I ARRIVED ON STRATTON ISLAND, MAINE, WITH TWO RUBBER-coated dry bags that I'd borrowed, never imagining they'd actually come in handy. The contents of the waterproof bags included a tent that I didn't know how to assemble and an assortment of clothes that were missing all the essentials. My choice of jeans and fleece turned out to be infelicitous, as I sat in the Zodiac, backpack on my knees, marinating in Atlantic brine for the entire fifteen-minute crossing. I immediately regretted my decision to forgo the knee-high rubber boots purchase, thinking that my water-proof hiking boots could withstand a week on the island.

Like the TV ads for Newfoundland that never featured a drop of rain, the photos I had seen from Audubon's Project Puffin featured volunteers with slightly sunburned faces and hardy bodies banding terns and other seabirds on rug-ged island terrain in ideal weather conditions. Although the website stressed variable and volatile weather, I couldn't see past the sun- and windswept island vistas in the photographs, especially in the one of a research assist-ant sitting atop a wooden structure, gazing off into the pink-hued sunset, taking in the otherworldly view from the field station. I imagined that said volunteer later went to bed exhausted, satisfied and at peace with her life choices.

I hadn't exactly imagined what would be involved in "rustic living" on an island without electricity. The last time I had slept in a tent was thirty years before. My childhood sleeping bag, green with orange-and-blue-checked flannel inside, had been a gift from our Canadian relatives, who operated under the erroneous assumption that my family might one day be interested in camping. My parents received a more attractive red-and-navy number. I remember using the sleeping bags once—to make a fort in the living room, under the coffee table. I had wanted to try sleeping outside, but my mother worried that my kidneys—and my woman parts, lurking in close proximity—would catch cold, and besides, what would the neighbours think of a child sleeping outside alone? The thought of a tent hadn't dawned on any of us, and the notion of backyard camping felt unsavoury. Hadn't we immigrated to Canada precisely in order to avoid vacationing in tents and sleeping bags? I last used that sleeping bag at a Zionist summer camp off the coast of Vancouver Island, during our annual three-day *tiyul*—a hiking and camping trip I loathed so much that I faked a sore ankle just so I could skip the hiking portion.

My parents neglected to introduce me to the natural world. I grew up in a house with five pianos and a twenty-volume set of Tolstoy's collected works resting on a Russian-only bookshelf next to my bed. By the age of five, I knew the name Anna Karenina, and by age seven I knew that her tragic fate involved a train. For fun, I memorized composers' birth and death dates, and I developed a crush on Franz Schubert, based on a drawing I had seen in one of his biographies. This was obviously an image of pre-syphilitic Schubert; he closely resembled Geordie Nicholson, my longstanding elementary school crush, against whose preternaturally good looks I measured all other humans. By age ten, I knew all about Van Gogh and his poor ear. I prided myself on being the only one in my Grade 5 class who had been to the Metropolitan Museum of Art and could differentiate between a Monet and a Manet. And yet I didn't know what a robin looked like. I didn't even know the bird existed. I had only encountered the word *Robin* as a last name, pertaining to a certain Christopher, dear friend of Winnie-the-Pooh, or *Vinniy Pukh*, as my parents referred to him in Russian. My childhood played out exclusively indoors.

IN 2016, A YEAR AFTER MY SUCCESSFUL BLACK-AND-WHITE warbler extraction from a mist net, I had gotten it into my head that I needed an adventure. I knew I couldn't manage a solo expedition in the wild; this adventure had to be on a diminutive scale, without any extreme physical exertion but still at the mercy of the elements. And so I decided to volunteer with Project Puffin—a seabird restoration initiative situated on eight islands off the coast of Maine. I had no idea what any of this meant but assumed that living on an uninhabited island among birds for as long as I could stand to be away from my husband would be a fantastic entry into a more authentic, embodied life.

I had come to nature through literature. I read and reread the hunting scenes in *Anna Karenina*, where Levin and Oblonsky go out with their retinue and dogs, and after an exhausting day of hunting snipe, they retreat into their lodges, drink tea from samovars and devour hearty meals. The hunts were moments of epiphany, in which characters felt lighter, in control, at one with something larger than themselves, and at a remove from the trappings of society. I wanted respite from the city, from my ordinary life. But what I didn't know was that I also—deeply—craved the samovar.

I started perusing Instagram feeds of biology fieldwork interns and wanted to dip into their existence. I started imagining my hair in a mop-like mess from a lack of showers, my face slightly sunburned, my fingernails dirty, my hands coarse. Before I even set foot on Stratton Island, I dreamt about it. I borrowed a sleeping bag from a friend, prepared my collection of Vermont-made woollens that would finally get a workout in their intended environment, bought a new notebook for the occasion, and considered myself ready for a collection of life-changing epiphanies. I was about to discover my place in the wild.

I READ THE WORDS *TENT, SLEEPING BAG* AND *ABILITY TO LIFT fifty pounds*, but none of them registered. I hadn't factored in living at the whim of weather.

I arrived on the island and was met by four conservation biologist interns, all in their early twenties. They showed me to a raised wooden platform for my tent, which I had no idea how to assemble. A few minutes later, I went in search of these intrepid souls, admitting my incompetence at tent assemblage, and before I knew it, I had posh, if leaky, accommodations, loosely protected by a tarp that inspired little confidence. Whether it was during the nautical-knot-tying process, which I faked by tying a glorified double knot, or shortly after, when it began to pour, I'm not sure, but I quickly began to question the substantiality of my wild side and the possibility that I didn't have one.

By the third day, I asked Miguel, a visiting intern from Mexico who spent entire field seasons living alone in a wilderness area, about his neck.

"Your neck doesn't hurt after sleeping on the ground?" I hadn't realized I'd be speaking Spanish on the island, and the smugness I felt when the idiomatic expression *no te duele* rolled off my tongue with ease quickly gave way to shame when I couldn't remember the word for *neck*. My vocabulary for body parts was rusty. I substituted *head* for *neck*, and took to miming everything I said, the way I used to do when I taught my second-year Russian class and knew that ample gesticulation compensated for lack of linguistic comprehension.

"I sleep better outside than I do at home. The mattress pad is more comfortable than my own bed."

"You're lucky. Mine is really flat."

"You mean you didn't inflate it?" And just to make sure I understood, Miguel cupped his hands over his mouth in a tube-shape and blew into it, with gusto. With a quick calculation, I realized that I'd last slept alfresco in 1985, a full decade before Miguel was born.

Without saying another word, Miguel followed me to my droopy-looking tent, where I silently handed him my mattress pad. He miraculously inflated it.

I might have come to fieldwork twenty years too late. The photos didn't prepare me for a downpour that nearly swept my tent off the ground. Nothing prepared me for the days that I spent drenched, unable to warm up no matter how many packages of hot cocoa I consumed, or the thunder and sideways rain, or the two nights when I slept in the expedition tent, too terrified to brave my own soaking palazzo; I lay in my sleeping bag staring at my surroundings in shock, sandwiched between the guns used for shooting black-crowned night herons—the notorious predators of the least tern chicks we were working hard to conserve—bird banding equipment, and plastic bins of data sheets and technical gear.

Where I suffered from meteorological malaise, the interns met island weather conditions with grace and fortitude. They were the very people in the photos I had coveted, the ones I thought I would become, only I lacked their *savoir faire* and their general good humour in the face of thunder, leaky tents, soggy sleeping bags and constantly wet feet. The four of them, who had already spent two months together, had become a tight unit with a language of their own.

THIS WASN'T MY FIRST TIME IN MAINE. LIKE MOST THINGS, I discovered Maine through literature. I read E.B. White's iconic essay, "Once More to the Lake," in high school and found myself longing for a place I hadn't yet seen. I connected with White's nostalgia for a bygone time. As soon as I had the chance, I applied to be a camp counsellor at OMNI Camp, in Maine. The summer after my freshman year, I travelled to Poland, Maine, in search of nature and adventure. I found it in the form of a cabin full of sixteen-year-old girls, most of whom looked older than me and would rather do anything other than listen to me. The outdoors paled in comparison to the full-blown wilderness in my cabin.

I spent evenings talking to a friend on a payphone, a friend who would become a boyfriend as soon as we next saw each other. Those conversations were filled with longing, promises and dreams, which only distance saved from ridicule. A few years later, the fellow with whom I spent countless hours talking from that payphone would come visit me in Providence, Rhode Island, where I went to university, and we would drive out to Maine over Thanksgiving, to relive those early days of our courtship. The end was already inscribed in the beginning: not only could we not locate the precise place from which I used to call him, but by then a strange silence had seeped into our conversations. I couldn't have known it back when we whispered and laughed into that payphone. And I couldn't have known that three years later we'd end up living together in Vancouver and that nothing would go as planned.

ON STRATTON ISLAND, WE WAITED OUT THE RAIN. SHANNON sat in her tent, which boasted a more protective tarp than mine, Frank and Coco read at the table in the wooden kitchen shelter, and I helped Jaime enter data from the previous day's productivity studies. Afterwards, I took refuge in the bird blind with Miguel.

"I think those are semipalmated plovers," I pointed out, thrilled that I could identify at least one shorebird. They performed their happy dance along the shore.

"Charadriidae family, definitely." Miguel referred to every species by its scientific name; ornithology in Latin America rarely relies on common names, since they differ in each Spanish-speaking country. "Ah, look over there, the beautiful *Pluvialis squatarola*, ready to breed. See the black stomach?"

I flipped through Sibley frantically, trying to match his description with the Latin binomial, and when I got to the page of plovers, Miguel tapped the black-bellied plover picture. There it was, with its jet-black belly plumage extending all the way up its neck, at the only time of year when the bird's name corresponded to its physique.

I counted. I marvelled. I saw so many common eiders that they no longer seemed interesting. I watched common terns dive-bomb any creature that came within reach of their chicks. I counted harbour seals as they lounged around, astounded by their lethargic style and their comfort and ease at doing absolutely nothing. I watched common tern chicks scurry about, nervously waiting for their parents to arrive and stuff their tiny mouths with fish, which they swallowed whole. I detected an oystercatcher walking along the shore, along with a willet and a greater yellowlegs. All of these shorebirds that I couldn't have identified mere weeks ago had become familiar to me, their names second nature. In the midst of the birdy mayhem, I could discern the whistling call of a killdeer, and knew it was the least sandpipers out there dotting the sand with their footprints—so light I had no idea how they withstood the wind. I learned to distinguish a greater from a lesser yellowlegs, and sat transfixed by the red feet of a black guillemot. The ruddy turnstones, with their rusty bellies, darted about in packs.

The island had four species of breeding terns—Arctic, common, roseate, and least—and we were there to survey the population of breeding pairs and to monitor their productivity and chick growth. One day, I sat in a blind with Coco for three hours, datasheets on our knees, trying to determine which species of tern consumed what kind of fish and how many of each they ingested. Since there were two of us, we got the deluxe blind—at one square metre, and a metre and a half high, it could fit two stools. Not only did all the fish seem identical to me no matter how diligently I studied the fish chart, but after about an hour even the terns became indistinguishable. Suddenly the faint rosy tinge on the underparts of the roseate tern was lost on me, and the roseate tern looked exactly like the common tern, which I could no longer tell apart from the Arctic tern, since from the blind everybody's legs looked uniformly short. I had studied Sibley and had memorized the descriptions for all three of the terns, but the field marks all began to meld into one. Who had the black tip on their red bill? Whose feet were shortest? Whose bill was mostly black but not entirely and turns orange at the end of the season and in the wrong light looks exactly like somebody else's bill? And when the terns are flying at breakneck speed, swerving, and diving...? Well, I ended up contenting myself with listening to Coco call out names of fish; by that point, my binoculars were pointed toward the horizon and I sat there, shocked that things looked, for the first time, exactly as I had imagined, at least meteorologically speaking.

In my desperate quest for adventure, I wanted nothing more than to live among birds. But now that I was there, I realized I didn't quite know how to be. The work in the blind required an attention to detail and an interest in the minutiae of which science is made, which I neither had nor knew how to acquire. What intrigued me more than what species consumed which fish at what rate was how Coco had discovered the wild, where she had camped, how she'd learned to tie nautical knots, and how she had backpacked through the canyons of New Mexico, walked through rivers and survived life in wet hiking boots for ten days. She answered my questions, but her eyes were glued to the birds. As mine ought to have been.

ONCE THE RAIN BROKE, WE WEIGHED THE LEAST TERN fledglings, and my job was to grab them as they scurried on the rocks. I watched the people I worked with just snatch the birds without thinking, without weighing the possibility of doing it wrong and hurting the bird, without wondering if they were in the right place, contemplating how this may or may not change their life, examining the human condition, and imprinting on their minds exactly how they would transmit this on paper. I watched Coco simply bend down, cup the darting bird in her hands and carry it to the bucket that held the assembled baby terns. She worked quickly and efficiently, and I followed her lead. Miguel stood by the bucket and reached his hand in to remove a tern, which he weighed by placing it in a bag and onto a scale, reading the weight and the band number on its right foot to Shannon, who recorded the data, before moving on to the next bird.

Without letting myself assume that I would injure the bird, I grabbed a least tern, felt its heartbeat in my hands, put it in bander's grip (by holding its head between my index and middle fingers), turned it on its side so I could read the band number, deposited it in a weighing sack, read out the number to the person recording numbers, and let the fledgling go.

The entire operation took no more than half an hour. There were six of us and about thirty terns scurrying about. We found a few dead ones. In that half-hour I had no time to question what I was doing; I simply ran after terns, grabbed them and carried them to the bucket, working fast lest I traumatize the birds.

On my last day on the island, I met Ali, a former volunteer who alighted on the island by kayak after the one-and-a-half-mile traverse from Prouts Neck.

"It only took forty minutes," she said as she emerged from the boat with a minuscule waterproof backpack that held her sleeping bag, iPhone, journal, toothbrush, sweater and wool leggings.

"You weren't scared?"

"Of what?"

"The crossing." I had only been in a kayak once, on Georgian Bay, and had managed to fall out.

"I didn't really think about it. I just wanted to see the least tern chicks. When I left three weeks ago, they hadn't hatched yet."

After introducing Ali to the chicks, most of which danced around the shoreline, hopping out of crags in the rocks, our supervisor, Frank, herded us out to the other side of the island for some invasive plant management. For two hours, we extracted weeds from the tall grasses growing amidst the rocks on the rugged beach. I felt good about pulling the thick grasses out three at a time—until I looked over at Ali, who was down on all fours in a tank top and short shorts, grabbing the weeds from their base and tugging vehemently, as if she were on a rowing machine. I watched as the mound of shorn grasses grew large around her feet and the scratches accumulated on her bare arms and legs; in the midst of hand-shearing grasses, I overheard her discussing Mexican seabirds with Miguel, in fluent Spanish. By the time Frank herded the troops back to the kitchen shelter, I was sitting on a rock, struggling to extract a splinter from my palm.

"Was this everything you had expected?" Frank asked.

"Nothing beats this view." I wasn't lying. Nor could I straighten my back after two hours of grass management duty. I'd had a vision of myself outdoors, living with birds, entirely divorced from technology and everyday life. I wanted to be a student of weather, dependent on the whims and fancies of nature. But I hadn't accounted for the fact that the whimsies of weather are often best read about from the comfort of one's couch, or the fact that I might be, at the very best of times, a bit of an armchair explorer.

That day also coincided with my turn to perform "dog" duty, which meant recording the temperature and wind direction at 6:00 a.m. and walking down the path to the central blind on the shore to count the common eiders, harbour seals, double-crested cormorants, gadwalls, great black-backed gulls, black guillemots, American oystercatchers and mallards. I stretched the morning observation count to take in the entire vista and watch the tide flowing in to create a bridge between our island and the rocks, replete with reclining seals. As dog, I also prepared dinner for our six-person team; since my dinner duty coincided with the last day before grocery shopping, I resorted to pasta with insipid tomato sauce, wilted broccoli and a side of guacamole, which would have been acceptable had Miguel not managed the impossible the night before, combining tomato sauce, cheese, tortillas, jalapeño peppers and a few other secret ingredients into an unsightly pile of mush that defied all expectations and had everybody requesting seconds. My pasta extravaganza left nobody asking for more, and I scooped the remains into the compost pile behind our makeshift kitchen.

I LEFT STRATTON ISLAND IN A HAZE, AND WHEN I ARRIVED at the airport in Boston, the last strands holding my trip together unravelled. I got there early, only to learn that my flight was delayed due to extreme heat on the tarmac in Indianapolis. What should have been a late-afternoon flight now promised to become an evening flight, and finally, by 10:00 p.m., the delay morphed into a cancellation. By that point I had befriended four other stranded travellers, and rather than part ways in favour of a night in a free hotel, we opted to make a camping experience of it, asked for cots and slept next to the luggage carousel on the deserted—and overly air-conditioned—arrival level. Not only did my new friends compliment my sleeping bag, but they marvelled at my fortitude and ability to sleep on any surface presented to me.

"Clearly, she must know a thing or two about the wild," my new friend Jacquie said to Micheline and Tony.

"Well, I just came back from a breeding tern colony," I said.

"A what?"

"Terns look a bit like seagulls, but they're a more elegant version. Anyhow, they nest and breed on islands off the coast of Maine and our job is to protect their nesting sites from predators, both human and animal."

"Are you a biologist?"

"No. I just love birds."

"So let me get this straight: you lived on an island without electricity for five days, and slept in a wet tent, all because you love birds?"

I nodded. I probably should have said something about the importance of conservation, the diverse habitat on twenty-four-acre Stratton Island—with rocky outcrops and ideal beach habitat for terns, as well as pygmy maritime deciduous forest that offers vital nesting habitat for shorebirds—or the specific work that Project Puffin has done to protect and restore species at risk. But I left it at that. Maybe that was it; maybe I was just motivated by love.

"You really are a wild one," Tony said. And then, shivering in his purple polo shirt, he rolled onto his back, tucked his feet into his flimsy WestJet blanket and stared at the fluorescent ceiling lights.

A Mistake Won't Kill You

IN AN OLD BLACK-AND-WHITE PHOTOGRAPH TAKEN BEFORE I
could walk, I'm seated at the piano in my Soviet woollens,
next to my mother, my pudgy fingers sinking into the
keys of the upright Ukraina-Chernigov. Tacit expectations
haunted my grandparents' purchase of this instrument for
my four-year-old mother in 1956: my mother's keen perfect pitch, and my grandmother's even more keen desire
to live out her own musical dreams vicariously, meant
that my mother was destined for a life of music. Even after
we left the Soviet Union, my grandparents still kept their
piano, even though they couldn't play it, as a reminder of
their only daughter, who had emigrated. We often received
photographs of them posing in front of the piano, paid for
in installments after an unaffordable bribe.

In 1984, as Vancouver prepared itself for Expo 86 and,
for the sixth year in a row, my grandparents were denied
exit visas to Canada, my parents transferred their energy
into the acquisition of a custom-made grand piano. Since
they couldn't determine when or if they would ever see
my grandparents, they poured their expectations into

this instrument, whose construction they meticulously supervised over the next two years. It was almost as if my mother had a presentiment that in the latest photograph we received of my grandfather, somewhere in his sad smile resided a seed of the cancer that would prevent her from ever seeing him again.

AS A CHILD IN VANCOUVER, INSTEAD OF VISITING GRANDPARents on the weekends, I visited a grand piano in Seattle. My parents had met a piano refurbisher whose devilish-sounding last name was a pseudonym, Manteufel, and whom they contracted to create a musical miracle for them—a nineteenth-century Bechstein with a modern soundboard crafted to their specifications. They chose the piano hammers and made sure that the action mechanism produced exactly the weight they wanted for each key, and we watched this beast of a piano transform before our eyes from a box-like structure into an actual instrument. We drove to Seattle every other weekend over the course of two years, to inspect every detail on the piano and to ensure that their savings—and borrowed money—wouldn't be wasted.

Obi Manteufel's warehouse had soundboards everywhere, along with piano keys, hammers, cast-iron plates and a few long-haired, aging dogs that lazed about on the floor. In the corner, next to a partially intact organ, he kept a makeshift kitchen with a coffee pot, a hot-plate and a mini-fridge. Though I later shattered my grandmother's dreams of having a granddaughter in the medical profession, the hours I spent in Obi's workshop were as close as I'd ever come to scientific pursuits. I imagined myself in a Renaissance anatomical theatre, the kind Rembrandt must have visited before painting his *Anatomy Lesson.* I followed keyboard dissections closely and collected data as I ambled through the piano-parts laboratory and transcribed vital statistics into my notebook: year of initial construction, measurements, state of decomposition, and salvaging potential. The pathology report made up for the long drive and the night spent in a sleeping bag on my parents' friend's floor.

Obi would often scream at his young, rosy-cheeked assistant, who did most of the carpentry work, as the three of us stared, thankful that his wrath avoided us. "He's a piano-making genius," my father would say, excusing Obi's latest outburst. Month after month, we returned.

I read *The Diary of Anne Frank* in Obi's warehouse, sitting in one of the paisley velour armchairs marked with cigarette burns and coffee stains. I sank into the chair, rolled my coat into a pillow and dangled my legs over one of the arms. When I kicked off my boots, my mother said, "As long as your feet don't touch the floor," pointing to the nails and scraps of wood scattered everywhere. The warehouse is where I thought about who might have owned that Bechstein in the nineteenth century, and whether it was a girl like me who was also forced to play the piano.

We drove the three-hour distance to Seattle in our aging Dodge Dart and I brought along my best clothes and favourite books, as if we were going to see old friends. Sometimes I would lie down on the sawdust-covered floor in my coat under a half-built piano and listen to the sounds emerging from a variety of pianos-in-progress. I loved the weekends because they freed me from any musical obligations. I could be among pianos and yet not have to touch a single one of them.

We celebrated the Bechstein's arrival at our home in Vancouver with a welcome party. The piano arrived with an entourage consisting of Obi, his carpenter companion and a piano tuner, Daryl, who emptied my parents' champagne bottle. My parents' most advanced students were invited for the event, and I sat in the corner of the basement studio, listening to them take turns playing Chopin's études and Liszt's Hungarian rhapsodies, and marvelling at the instrument's unexpected range and perfectly calibrated sound.

Later, when we moved to Toronto, the piano didn't fit in our apartment building's elevator, and we hired a crane to lift it to the fifth floor and load it in through the balcony door. I remember my mother watching the spectacle, her hand covering her mouth, breathing heavily, and my father standing next to her, mouth agape while the unrecognizable piano, covered in layers of packing blankets, wobbled slightly from side to side. Their entire savings were wrapped up in what looked like a rectangular box from above. My parents invited Daryl to visit us, and he banged out chords and intervals while adjusting the pegs with this tuning device for hours—until the neighbours threatened to call the management company. The piano resided in the dining area and dwarfed our table, which my parents had relegated to a corner of the room.

When I moved back to Toronto, they bought a Steinway that slowly eclipsed the Bechstein. Steinways are more predictable; most concert halls have Steinways, and it's easier for performers to anticipate the demands of a concert grand if they have a similar piano at home. It made sense, but I didn't understand. I remembered the wanting, the waiting, the hoping, the craving, the sense of expectation: the certainty that this was it, the piano my parents had been waiting for their entire lives. The shift unsettled me, and at the same time I envied their way of adapting to a situation and simply moving on. I'm the one who remains nostalgic for an instrument that I was never good enough to play to its potential.

I GREW UP WITH THE WORKS OF VIENNESE COMPOSER AND pianist Carl Czerny, and to me he was always a sign of the thing I would never be able to do: I didn't play his studies fast enough, and even the sound I teased out from the piano wasn't enough. They were always a step beyond me.

But now that I'm becoming a birder, I've come back to Czerny. I bought his *School of Velocity*, the dreaded op. 299, which will one day, hopefully, lead me to the even more dreaded, faster, more challenging op. 740, the *Art of Finger Dexterity*. I can't tell you whether I am getting faster or better—of course I am, but it's hard to tell with incremental process, when you're in the thick of it—but I love the very thing I couldn't stand as a younger student: the repetition, the feeling of muscle memory kicking in when my fingers know exactly where to go, the sense that my fingers can instinctively apply what I've practised in Czerny to a Schubert impromptu or a Beethoven sonata.

When I turn to Czerny now, it's the words *velocity* and *dexterity* that I latch onto—as if he knew that these precise skills would help me extract birds from mist nets, as if he knew that they would speak to my new life with birds.

I no longer practise piano with an end-goal in mind. I passed my ARCT (the Royal Conservatory's Associate Diploma) exam back in 1996, and received my performance certificate. So what do I practise for now? I don't perform in public, but I'm at the piano for almost an hour every day, hammering my way through a study, roaming around in a Brahms intermezzo. As with birding, I'm in it for the process of getting from one note to another, from one modulation to another. I started learning Schubert impromptus because I remember hearing my father play them as I grew up. I poke around in pieces of music the way I read books—both are a way of parsing the sound.

I hear my childhood in every Czerny study I learn. I used to practise upstairs, often with a book resting open on my knees, hoping my mother wouldn't notice, but her perfect pitch never deceived her. "Wrong note!" she yelled from the kitchen. What I didn't know then, and what would have made me more sympathetic to Czerny, was that not only was he a technical genius, but he had been Beethoven's most famous student. Beethoven had even asked him to teach his beloved nephew, Karl. When Beethoven could no longer hear or perform his work in public, he turned the task over to Czerny. The Vienna premiere of Beethoven's "Emperor" concerto in 1812 had Carl Czerny seated at the piano.

For the first forty-nine years of his life, Czerny taught for twelve hours a day—Franz Liszt remains his most famous student—and then he abandoned his teaching for a career in composition and wrote 861 numbered works, of which virtually nothing but the technical studies are played, though never performed in public. Czerny is a force with which every pianist is intimate, and though there have been renaissance movements, reappraisals and critical studies of him by noted musicologists, his pieces remain a private affair: a mountain that every pianist contends with, alone. Had I known that the God of Piano Technique, my childhood nemesis, fought battles of his own to build a legacy that never quite materialized, I might have been more sympathetic.

NOW THAT I'M BIRDING, ALL I DO IS PRACTISE. EVERYTHING I do is a form of practice because the only way to recognize a bird is to look at it and look at it and look at it again, and misidentify it and return to the field guide, and misidentify it some more, and talk through your mistake with other birders, and examine the bird in detail, and Google "difference between white-breasted nuthatch and chickadee" when you feel particularly idiotic, and finally realize that the posture of a nuthatch would be impossible for a chickadee, and somewhere around the eightieth misidentification, something clicks and you see a nuthatch exactly for what it is and wonder how even the day before you might have confused it with a chickadee. Could I really have been such an idiot?

If nothing else, birding is the art of practice, coupled with patience. A few months ago, I plugged away at a Czerny study for twenty minutes every day, and for the first two weeks I stumbled in the same places, my chromatic scales achy, lopsided, barrelling toward the last bar, hoping for the best and failing every time. I walked away from the piano a few times, knowing full well that my parents' ten-year-old students could play this faster, lighter, better than I ever would. And the next day, I was back on the piano bench, and when I stopped to listen to myself, I had to admit that though the chromatic scale still stalled in a few places, the pace had picked up, and somehow instead of playing in groupings of four notes, I was already up to eight. I couldn't have managed this incremental accretion even ten years ago—I didn't yet have the patience.

Or, it's as my ballet teacher says, "What—are you afraid of making a mistake? It won't kill you, you know." Puzzling through birdsong, getting a headache while trying to pick out the nuances of the difference between a dark-eyed junco's and a pine warbler's song—one of them has a faint hint of a trill, and though I couldn't tell you which one, the only saving grace is that they rarely appear at the same place at the same time—has inadvertently brought me back to music. What I once considered boring and insurmountable now entices me to try again, try a little harder, listen a little closer.

The Twitch

I'VE BEEN TOYING WITH THE IDEA OF BUYING A FOLD-UP bicycle for the accidental arrival of a rarity at Tommy Thompson Park. I love the idea of a car-free five-kilometre urban wilderness peninsula in downtown Toronto, but when a bird appears three kilometres into the shade-free park on a day when the humidex is so high you stop consulting the weather app, you begin fantasizing about bikes. I had that exact experience two summers ago when the tricoloured heron graced Toronto with a historic landing. I got the bird, but nearly collapsed in the process; full of envy of the birders who had cycled into the park, virtually sweat-free, and found the bird within fifteen minutes of arriving, I wanted what they had.

My birthday was coming up. What does one buy for one's forty-third birthday? It's neither here nor there. My fortieth involved the purchase of an enormous recliner to ease the transition into the new decade. It didn't help the relentless anxiety, nor did it magically turn back the clock, which was the gift I'd secretly been hoping for, but it did make for more comfortable evenings. Turning forty-one and forty-two were hardly memorable, and I decided that forty-three needed something to mark the occasion, not because I saw the number as auspicious but just because I craved something and had no idea what.

The day I saw Lynne Freeman, president of the Ontario Field Ornithologists, ride into the bird banding station on her fold-up bicycle, I knew exactly what I wanted. Her poise was regal, and I started imagining my life as the owner of a fold-up bicycle. I started envisioning a new chapter. A rare-bird chapter.

It's hard to understand this twitching business. A rare bird shows up, you receive an e-mail alert and suddenly you're off in search of whatever vagrant has happened to grace your geographic locale.

I still struggle to describe the feeling of seeing a rare bird to someone who isn't a birder.

"I saw a rare bird yesterday," I tell my sister.

"Oh. That's great."

"A fork-tailed flycatcher. All the way from South America." I said. "That bird had no business being in Toronto yesterday."

Silence.

"It is a one-day wonder."

"No, really, that's great."

"You don't care about the fork-tailed flycatcher, do you?"

"I'm riveted."

She humours me. Even though we're talking on the phone, I know she's giving me that look. There's a particular look that I get from my family. It's vaguely similar to the look I used to give them as a sullen teenager, when they picked me up and I had to watch them interact with my friends. The I-can't-quite-believe-we-belong-to-the-same-species look.

The first time I remember giving my father that look was just after Madonna had released "Material Girl."

"Papa, who's Madonna?"

"She is the mother of Jesus Christ," my dad said. "Where did you hear about her?"

"At school. Andrea is dressing up as Madonna for Halloween."

"Interesting. Nice that Canadian children are taking an interest in religion." That night, he showed me paintings of Renaissance and medieval Madonnas in the art books he and my mother had recently begun to collect.

After I'd made a fool of myself at school the next day, I told my dad, "You told me about the wrong Madonna."

"There's another one?"

"She just released an album called *Like a Virgin*." I giggled at the word *virgin* and followed the statement with a look, in response to which my father shrugged.

I'VE LONG PRIDED MYSELF ON MODERATION. I MOCKED MY husband for the way he played badminton with a leg injury. "It's a game," he said, which translates into "you play until you can't move any longer." And even then, moderation is diametrically opposed to sports, he told me, because there you push yourself to the limit. None of his talk about limits and pain made sense to me.

The twitch is different. I read the ONTBIRDS listserv with trepidation; I'm nervous that I'll find something irresistible. I'm scared it will make me jump in my car, no matter the weather, no matter the traffic, no matter the distance. There's nothing reasonable about a twitch. It takes over your mind and body, and off you go, in search of a bird. Usually it's a bird that's in your neck of the woods by accident, through meteorological confusion or a lost sense of direction, or an error in judgment. You never even knew that you wanted to see it.

IN JUNE 2017, A SCISSOR-TAILED FLYCATCHER SPENT A DAY near Toronto, and I missed it. For the third time. I had expected the bird to stick around for a couple of days, but it turned out to be a one-day wonder. I missed it because I was tired, having just come back from work, and the last thing I wanted to do was hop in my car and head for Mississauga, where the bird was hanging out in a shrub, posing for photographers and birders alike, merrily fooling us all into believing that he'd be there for a few days at least, so co-operative and relaxed appeared his posture. And so I turned off my computer, calmly ate dinner and planned my next day's outing, when I could see the bird on my own terms.

And here is where nature mocks you absolutely. Birds don't work on your schedule. They don't care an iota for your plans or your desires. They ridicule your fantasy that you are in control of what it is you see. They appear when they want to and disappear accordingly.

Fast-forward three months to the appearance of a fork-tailed flycatcher. I was at the banding station when a friend received an update on her phone. Toronto was enduring a peculiar heat wave in September. Nothing functioned normally, the birds were late to migrate south, and we closed nets early because of the thirty-two-degree heat and accompanying humidity. I stopped to look for the bird on my way out of the park, but I couldn't find it and decided to return the following day, with water and with more patience. How special could a fork-tailed flycatcher be, anyhow?

And then I came home and checked eBird. Not only had the bird been found within minutes of my leaving, but the photos defied human imagination. This wanderer from the tropics must have made a massive navigation mistake. He did not belong in Toronto, yet here he was. The bird resembled a more elegant version of an eastern kingbird with a colossally long tail that forked into the splits when it flew. I couldn't have imagined a bird like this—it looked like a potential close relative of the Firebird, which I knew from Russian fairy tales.

A twitch isn't something you can stop. It's a compulsion, a necessity, an obsession. I'm not much of a lister, but I do fall in love with certain birds.

I spent a few hours weighing the pros and cons of driving all the way back to Tommy Thompson Park, and then biking all the way in.

"Isn't this exactly the reason why you bought your fold-up bike?" Leon said. "What did you call that other one you missed? A one-day wonder?"

Leon knew that if I missed this bird, he'd be consoling me about this humiliating dip for months to come. He carried my fold-up bike down to my car and shooed me out the door at six o'clock.

"Don't come home without the bird!" he threatened.

I biked into the park, passing birders walking slowly, with scopes on their shoulders, and followed the crowd into the path leading to Cell 1. There was no missing this bird; half of the southern Ontario birding world got the memo and made a beeline for Tommy Thompson Park. And there he was, perched atop a shrub, looking monumentally out of place. Over and over, I watched him show off his long, remarkably nimble forked tail as he looped in the air. I couldn't take my eyes off him.

The bike saved me the day I saw the fork-tailed flycatcher. And so did Leon, since it did, in fact, end up being a one-day-wonder sighting. It wasn't just about putting the bird on my list. It was about knowing that I was among the happy few to be in the right place at the right time. For me, twitching isn't about the numbers. It's about being privy to something out of the ordinary—a fortuitous accident of nature. It's an induction into a rarefied world.

Celebrity Bird

BIRDING HAS CHANGED MY PERCEPTION OF TIME. THE CAL-endar now operates on different terms for me. I feel a sense of excitement every spring when I see warblers for the first time; I recognize a few more of them every year. And the fall? Well, it's not only a letdown, it's downright depressing. In a sense, I feel abandoned. I feel a sense of promise in the spring. In the fall, the birds stop singing, for the most part, except for the occasional confused robin or red-winged blackbird who sings their heart out in the hope of one last hurrah. Their songs—due to autumnal recrudescence, when birds start feeling that urge all over again because light levels are in line with early spring—feel out of place and have a plaintive ring to them. There's no way around it: the days are getting shorter, and things are coming to a standstill.

As the birds fly south, I come to terms with my own mortality. It brings it one step closer. My parents are getting older. My grandmother will not be there forever. Every fall, I notice changes in myself, in my husband. Everything is okay, but there's a nervous sense of what-if-ness.

And then the Novemberness of things creeps in. The darkness looms, the days get shorter, and it feels like a long time till spring.

TWO YEARS AGO, TO CELEBRATE THE END OF THE SEASON, the banding station held its last owl night. Everybody brought food, and the atmosphere was festive, yet it was also the end of a season. The beginning of winter, the end of the songbirds. We set up the nets for the last time and I got a chance to use my headlamp, the one I had bought for my wild trip to Maine. It felt like I was clad in reminiscences—of a trip gone not quite right. And the evening began. In between mouthfuls of chips, we checked the nets. They were mostly empty. And then, shortly after nine o'clock, we caught a northern saw-whet owl. Tangled, he played dead while my friend Lynda extracted one wing and then the other, and finally his head from the net. The owl closed his eyes and gave himself up to us. Soon he was weighed and measured. I wrote down all the data, and I realized it was one of the last times I would scribe that year.

What do I love so much about scribing? I watch the birds as they're weighed and measured, as we puzzle through the aging and sexing process. Sometimes it's straightforward, other times we resort to Peter Pyle's inscrutable tome about banding North American birds and attempt to decipher his directions. It's a privileged position, to see the bird up close, to watch it breathing and opening and closing its eyes.

I believe in birds. I believe in their beauty, in their wisdom. I love the way they take me out of myself and enable me to live anew. I marvel at their capacity for flight, their sense of direction, their straightforward life, stripped down to the basics: eat, choose a mate, breed, protect. I gather that they don't think too much. They don't have writer's block. They don't sit around wondering what project to take on next; they don't worry about authenticity or presenting their best selves on social media. I love birds because their lives are nothing like mine, because my anxieties would not only seem inane to them but would register as a foreign language.

NIGEL GREETS US AT THE STATION, HIS HANDS SCRATCHED and bloodied. "A northern shrike," he says, and I know exactly what he means. He had banded a shrike earlier that day and the butcher bird nearly won the battle. Nobody uses gloves—the personal injuries are often a mark of pride.

At the banding station we laugh. We scroll through bird photos, exchange sightings, boast about best looks, discuss who's getting what where. We fantasize about places we would travel to see a bird, to band a bird, to hold a bird. The world becomes both extremely narrow in its focus and capacious in its possibility. Birds have no borders—their migratory paths aren't dictated by geopolitical situations. Birds are motivated by food and sex. It's that basic. In the banding station, we are focused on personal experience with plumage. Our bird sightings become extensions of ourselves, our passions. We talk about our families sometimes. It's a world of pliers, variously sized bands, a binder filled with data, a scale. Bronwyn's ghost looms large.

We forget about the vagaries of weather. It doesn't matter how cold it is, or whether the place has been flooded and we have to manoeuvre our way to the nets in hip waders with carp swimming around our feet.

We relish bird puns that never get old. When I'm scribing the data for a veery, Nigel will invariably walk by and say, "It's *veery* nice!" I remember the time I got my first bird joke, without requiring explanatory notes, which had usually been provided to me by Brete. I was scribing and marvelling at a feisty winter wren, whose perfectly erect, yet diminutive, tail stuck out at a sharp right angle from the torso. The tail had a life of its own, and someone walked by and said, "That looks like a winter wren crossed with a ruddy duck!" It wasn't the earth-shattering subtlety of the joke that startled me, but the fact that I understood it. I could picture the ruddy duck's signature erect tail, and I grasped the nuance of the entire reference; suddenly, I had access to new grammatical possibilities—like a new language learner parsing sentences, groping my way toward meaning. After years of reading, observing, scribing, listening, making mistakes, almost giving up—I found new, expansive, electrifying meaning.

We count. We tally. We mark time by bird sightings. We relish every Celebrity Bird we can remember. We forget pieces of our lives at the banding station. I'm forever leaving behind my boots or my binoculars case. Lisa leaves her prescription meds. There's a red vest floating about. We're there for the birds, for the data, but we're also there for ourselves.

"Being here makes everything better," Sarah says.

WE CHECKED THE NETS EVERY THIRTY MINUTES, EVEN though they all came up empty. And then at 11:40 p.m., shortly before I had to leave, I decided to accompany Denise on one last net-round. She had recently retired from a career in medicine, about twenty years earlier than she'd planned, on account of an immune disease, and we talked about health, about reconfiguring our lives, about how birds were helping us cope. And as we walked to the penultimate net on the north side of the station, we saw something flapping in the lowest shelf of the net. Denise grabbed it and I held the net in place so the bird could not get away.

"It's a huge female. Just look at it!"

"That's the biggest saw-whet I've ever seen."

"Definitely a female." Female birds might be drabber than their male counterparts, but in the raptor universe, they're always considerably larger.

We brought the bird back to the station, and when Nigel saw the owl's head, his face lit up.

"Holy shit, that's no saw-whet, that's a male eastern screech!" He said, repeating "eastern screech" at least five times, each time accompanied by a more colourful profanity. There is no shortage of emotion at the banding station, especially when we get a bird that's a first for the station.

The stocky greyish owl with pointed ear tufts had bright yellow eyes and seemed almost neckless. Everybody took turns taking selfies with it. Since I was scribing, I had the best view of his striped wings and his formidable neck twists, and I like to think that I locked eyes with the screech owl for a second longer than everybody else. Just when things had come to a standstill and I didn't anticipate a single other owl, we ended up having a record-breaking night: a Celebrity Bird of the Day and a station first.

THE END OF BANDING SEASON IS THE STRANGEST TIME, AND I think everybody's mind begins to wander. I think about the end of many of my other seasons, about not being a parent, about every way in which this year didn't quite match up to my expectations. But then, out of nowhere, a screech owl interrupts everything. And suddenly nobody is cold, nobody feels tired, and the night is young, with many, many seasons still ahead.

Birdsplainer in Training

I RECEIVED A MESSAGE ON TWITTER FROM MY FRIEND Lindsay, telling me that her mother had just seen a red-headed woodpecker at her feeder. She lives in Toronto, so the probability of such a bird appearing at one's feeder is close to non-existent. Without thinking, I responded immediately: "Likely not a red-headed woodpecker but a red-bellied woodpecker, even though it does have a red head."

And then I wondered, when had I become a birdsplainer? I've been birding for ten years and I still consider myself a beginner. When I'm out with birders who can identify species by ear, I'm embarrassed by my glaring mistakes. Just when I thought I'd internalized the high-pitched repetitive call of a northern flicker, for instance, it turned out that I had confused the song with an American robin, which is particularly humiliating because the calls usually sound nothing alike. Every time I think I've learned all the variations of the most common songsters, I'm shocked to find that there's another, slightly less common one lurking in their repertoire. And yet here I was, pontificating with great authority over Twitter. What ashamed me most was the tone I used; with a hint of smugness, I was proclaiming knowledge from the rafters.

A few weeks later, one morning in mid-April, I found myself at Colonel Samuel Smith Park, searching for American woodcocks that had been reported in the park. I quickly met two birders who were after the same species and off we went, hopping over a log and heading toward the creek.

"Did you know that woodcocks have eyes that can see backwards?" I asked.

"No."

"So that they can see prey coming at them."

"I think that's one flying over there," the birder with the long-lensed camera said to his friend, who sported an even longer-lensed one.

"Their bills also have nerve receptors that help them locate food." I couldn't stop. I wanted to regale them with the factoids I'd amassed through my reading, but by this point the birders with classy cameras were talking between themselves about things that had nothing to do with wood-cock trivia, perhaps afraid that I'd continue to shower them with information.

We parted ways without so much as a goodbye. They weren't satisfied with the looks they'd gotten and decided to try another vantage point. Part of me wondered if they were also sick of my oversharing. Either way, I ended up alone among at least four perfectly camouflaged wood-cocks that frequently erupted from the piles of leaves in haphazard flight patterns. I wanted to point out a foraging bird that would have made a great photo, but my almost-friends were long gone.

"I MET TWO BIRDERS AND I THINK I TALKED TO THEM TOO much," I said to my husband.

"Did you tell them everything you knew about woodcocks?"

"Pretty much."

"Had they asked?"

"Not exactly, but I just assumed they wanted to know."

"It's not a test, you know."

"I was just so excited to know *something*." I didn't tell Leon that I'd stopped right before telling them that the woodcock was my spirit animal. I did think that might be overstepping.

What was happening to me? I couldn't stop talking about birds.

But I didn't want to put people to sleep with my birdy explanations. I wanted to get people excited, show them something exquisite for the first time, and eventually make them fall so much in love with these birds that they'd want to help protect them.

I thought back to the most effective ways I've been taught about birds. On a birding trip to Monhegan Island, Maine, in 2013, I ended up on a bird walk one afternoon led by Peter Vickery. The walk ran three hours longer than planned because we happened upon tree after tree dripping with fall warblers. Since I still couldn't identify most of what I saw, I tried to excuse my inadequacy by using Roger Tory Peterson's famous term, "confusing fall warblers," to which Peter turned to me and said, "I wish he'd never said that."

I had never heard anybody contradict Roger Tory Peterson. His name alone represented sacred territory, and most of his quotes were proverbial.

"He really did a disservice to birders," Peter said. "Because he made fall warblers seem harder than they are." "But they all look the same," I said. "That's because you aren't really looking. What about the black-and-white? Parula? Black-throated green? Black-throated blue? Those ones are all the same spring and fall." I hadn't ever stopped to think of it, but he was right. Of the twenty-five or so common eastern warblers, fewer than ten honestly merited the label "confusing." The rest of them looked as they did in the spring, perhaps marginally drabber. "Peterson gave people an excuse to give up on fall warblers. It's a real shame."

I misidentified the Nashvilles and the blackpolls, but I started seeing the simpler ones for exactly what they were, rather than throwing up my hands and assuming the whole enterprise was beyond my ability. By the end of the walk, it was just Peter and me, and when he realized just how much of a beginner I was, he told me to forgo the rarities and instead pay close attention to the common backyard birds in my neighbourhood, learning their songs. "Rarities come and go," he said, "but the common birds will give you a base that you can then add to." He spoke to me as if he himself were just starting out and had difficulty distinguishing between a downy woodpecker and a yellow-bellied sapsucker.

On returning home, I Googled Peter Vickery and was stunned to learn that he was one of Maine's top birders. Yet he had never once birdsplained. Instead, he put himself in my shoes and gave me level-appropriate pieces of information. And I remembered all of it.

Last year I read an obituary for Peter Vickery online; I had wanted to e-mail him to tell him about my birding progress and how much his insight had changed the way I birded. I regret that I'll never get to send that e-mail, but I'm perhaps saddest that I'll never be able to tell him about the time four years ago when, thinking of him, I decided not to give up on a washed-out fall-plumage warbler. I walked ahead of my group, binoculars pointed upward, and took the time to look closely at the bird's defining field marks. I was so engrossed in coming up with the correct ID that I didn't realize I was walking and staring up through my binoculars at the same time. The moment I shouted "Blackburnian!" coincided with my fall into a construction well. By some miracle, I emerged from the well completely unscathed, save a few bruises, and I now wonder whether Peter Vickery had been looking out for me.

IT WAS HARD FOR ME TO REALIZE THAT MEETING PEOPLE IN the field didn't require me to lay out all my knowledge before them. Instead, I could look with them. I didn't have to convince anybody that I belonged out there. What was I compensating for? Why did I need to prove myself to people I didn't even know? I wanted to show them how much I loved birds, how interested I was, how much knowledge I had amassed, that I was a beginner who was still worthy of their time. I desperately wanted to appear smart.

So I birdsplained to prove myself.

I BOUGHT MY FIRST PAIR OF BINOCULARS IN NEW YORK. WE had gone during Passover and stayed an extra day to make sure that B&H was open. Overhead conveyer belts carried high-end optics all over the store, and I walked a few steps behind our salesman, an Orthodox Jew named Shloyme, as he showed me various models. I settled on the Zeiss Conquest HD.

"You're going to pay over a thousand dollars for binoculars?"

"They're worth it. Zeiss."

"German-made, yes? They were good with precision." And he gave me a good long stare. We both knew what he meant. Afterwards, he sneezed, wiped his nose with the back of his hand, and presented me with me my binoculars. I only hoped I had the skill to use them. This was an investment. Was I ready for it? I still had trouble focusing when I saw movement in a tree and needed to get the glasses on the bird quickly. I hadn't immediately thought of Zeiss. Initially, I had planned to get a pair of Vortex binoculars, the next grade up from Slade's Bausch & Lomb binoculars, which I still used, but I met a birder at Thickson's Woods, an hour's drive east of Toronto, who owned a pair of Zeiss Victory HTs and let me try them while we searched for a great horned owl. We never did find the owl, but the minute I brought the binoculars to my eyes and saw how much light they let in, I knew I wanted them.

I get no greater joy than from walking around with my binoculars. I try to log as many hours as I can. It used to be just Saturday mornings. Then I discovered a park a few kilometres away and added a weekday morning. On Sunday, Leon humours me and we go birding together, which means I birdsplain and stress about not seeing as many birds as a good birder would see.

"What's that bird up there?" he asks, pointing to something I can't see because of our difference in height.

"Where?"

"Over there. Just stand here, you'll see."

And I tell him that's a classic novice error. I teach him to give bird directions on a clock so that I will actually know what he's talking about. I teach him to describe the shape of branches so that I will have more reference points. By the time I get my glasses on the bird it has flown and I'm furious.

"How could we have missed it?"

"It must have been a really rare one," he teases.

Inside, I'm freaking out, wondering if he would love me more if I had more knowledge.

"I don't care what you know or don't know about birds. I just like being out with you," Leon tells me, and I am slowly learning to believe him.

SOMETIMES I JOKE THAT BIRDS SAVED MY LIFE. AND THEN I rephrase: birds gave me a new life, the one I never knew I needed, but exactly the one I wanted. To be among birds is to be constantly learning—about their history, biology, behaviour, plumage and migratory paths, and about ways to advocate on their behalf and help protect them. And although I'm most definitely a lifelong beginner birder, there's no place I'd rather be.

For the Nuances of Waterfowl

I SAID TO MY HUSBAND A LITTLE WHILE AGO, "I THINK IT might be time."

"You're ready to commit?"

"I don't see the point in waiting any longer." And with that I began a weight-training regimen in earnest. Alternating bicep curls, lateral raises, one-arm rows, shoulder presses, dumbbell bench press and tricep kickbacks—all with three-pound weights in each hand. Compared with my previous regimen of simply staring at the weights, this felt positively Olympic.

I was training for a spotting scope—or, in regular birding parlance, a scope. The weight of the scope itself is manageable, but the necessary accoutrements include a tripod and a protective case, all of which I would have to be able to carry on my back for miles. I've seen hardy birders fling their scopes over their shoulders with panache, but that isn't in the cards for me. I worry I'll end up somehow getting tangled in the scope. For someone with a weak back, like me, the process of acquiring the strength and fortitude to carry any significant weight quickly turned into a serious calisthenics project.

LEON AND I HAVE NEVER SEEN EYE TO EYE ON EXERCISE. I'VE always been of the moderation school of working out, which mostly means never working out in any form more aggressive than morning walks. Leon, on the other hand, discovered weightlifting as a teenager and prefers to push his body to maximum exhaustion. Early in our relationship, he had visions of us going to the gym as a couple. He graciously included me in his biceps workout; while I did the dumbbell bench press with five pounds in each hand, he held sixty pounds in each hand. Everything I did irritated him.

"Why are you yawning?"

"I don't know. Exercise just makes me tired. Maybe it's the lack of oxygen."

"This is a gym, not a library." I had made the mistake of telling him that I sometimes fell asleep in the library.

"Can you do the exercises without grunting?"

"I'm trying to fit in," I said.

"There's no danger of that, don't worry." Our romantic gym excursions lasted no more than a few months. He saw that I was happier with leisurely swims and long walks outside. But he didn't exactly give up. When he bought himself a set of kettlebells ranging from 35 to 110 pounds, he also bought me a diminutive 10-pound kettlebell and placed it next to the more serious equipment.

"You'll never feel stronger if you don't exercise," he told me when I slouched.

And I tried. Occasionally I lifted the kettlebell. Sometimes I did the weightlifting routine Leon had designed for me, but after three days I would lose interest. Months would go by, then I'd try again. The same pattern would ensue. I tried to find a sport that suited my personality, but it was a challenge. I carry Oblomovitis—the peculiar nineteenth-century Russian condition brilliantly evoked by Ivan Goncharov in his novel *Oblomov* and largely entailing lying on the couch in one's bathrobe and daydreaming for years on end—as cultural baggage. With that kind of literary ancestor, how could Leon possibly expect me to embrace vigorous exercise? Left to my own devices, my recliner is exactly the place to which I gravitate. It turned out that I was lacking a tangible goal.

WHEN THE TUFTED DUCK, AN OLD WORLD BIRD, TURNED UP in the greater Toronto area in 2017, the bird world went bananas. Some well-known birders in the area said they had waited seventeen years for the duck to show up. Every time I went out to see it, I missed it. The duck looks like a cross between a ring-necked duck and a greater scaup but has a dainty, if superfluous, tuft of hair dangling behind its head. In windy weather, the tuft takes on a life of its own and seems to follow the duck at a right angle. But in normal weather, it just hangs limply. The whole tuft business reminded me of the rat-tail hairdo I proudly donned in 1985, which my old-school Russian teacher cut off before I could even tell her how popular it made me seem at school. Just like that, she lopped it off, condemning the tail as decadent nonsense. And with it went my unrealized popularity.

I like to think I almost saw the tufted duck with my friend Martha, but really all we saw was a thousand or so greater scaup. My eyes glazed over, and all the scaup looked identical through my binoculars. My feet froze. It wasn't until I scanned through Martha's scope that I could detect some redheads, common goldeneye and a lone white-winged scoter in the bunch. Returning to my binoculars felt like a letdown after the scope. Once again, all I could see were scaup.

For two months, I started every day by reading the bird reports, but every tufted duck sighting happened when I had something non-negotiable scheduled. I also began to notice that almost every report began with "excellent scope views" or ended with "bird quite far from shore, best seen with a scope." I began to lose hope. Even if I did get to see the bird, I probably wouldn't actually *see* it.

"If it looks like a cross between your scaup and the duck with the whale on its side then just look in your field guide and say you saw it," Leon suggested.

"I'm glad you remember the trademark of the ring-necked duck," I said, "but it's not the same. I want a perfect look at the tufted duck. And a field guide sighting isn't the same as seeing the real thing."

"But you said yourself that even if you see it you won't get a good look at it."

"I need a scope."

"So buy one." We'd had this conversation before. My vision for Leon's early retirement included more couple's birding outings where he would carry my scope for me. His vision differed. "But I won't carry it for you."

THE DAY I PULLED OUT MY DUMBBELLS AND RESURRECTED my exercise routine, I had just seen the tufted duck. It happened accidentally. I had decided to stop trying for the duck, due to my combined lack of luck and lack of scope, but I went out birding anyhow. On a whim, I decided to check the trees in the Woodland Cemetery for a red-phased eastern screech owl, and I found it, thanks to bumping into an acquaintance who pointed me to the correct tree. Just as I was leaving, I ran into a photographer who suggested that I make a beeline for Hamilton, because Mr. Tuft had just reappeared at Windermere Basin. Instead of providing specific directions, he said, "Just look for the thirty scopes!" And I was off.

I arrived to find a miraculous scene. At the edge of the basin, where it narrows under a bridge, within clear binocular vision, the tufted duck swam amidst greater scaup, ruddy ducks and ring-necked ducks. I couldn't take my eyes off this dainty thing, which had somehow been blown off course or had mistaken southern Ontario for the Alaskan coastline. His tuft bobbed in the wind and I felt like I had won the lottery on a day when I hadn't even planned to buy a ticket. I had gone out to see the bird four times, unsuccessfully, and this felt like vindication.

Then I saw the bird through a scope and it came alive. The tuft danced gracefully in the air with a lightness that reminded me of everything I strive to capture in my *port de bras* in ballet class. The bird's bill looked like it had been dipped in black calligraphy ink, and his sparkling white sides like he'd been scrubbed clean by my mother-in-law's hand. This bird was no follower; he had his own agenda. I didn't want to overstay my welcome on someone else's scope and returned to observing him through my binoculars, where he remained utterly fantastic, but no longer the wonder of nature he'd been under hyper-magnification.

THE MORNING AFTER MY FIRST DUMBBELL ROUTINE, MY chest and back muscles felt like I'd been stretched by a medieval torture device. My husband smiled when I complained, and said nothing. I did the routine again. And again. Every time I wanted to quit, I though back to the tufted duck and picked up the dumbbells again, even if it was the last thing I did before bed.

I'm giving myself a year to acquire some dorsal muscle mass. I'm already noticing incremental changes in my body. Swimming has become easier and my backpack no longer feels so unspeakably heavy. I've shared my fitness goal with Martha and Monika, to make it feel more real.

"How's the regimen?" Martha asks.

"I want to be ready by next year."

"You can do it. And then you can watch shorebirds with me!"

"I'm actually doing it for the nuances of waterfowl." Martha gets it. When she bought her scope four years ago, she actually took it to bed with her. She recently started window-birding in her new lakefront condo, where she set up a scope in the den. She happily reported that not only can she tell a greater from a lesser scaup, but she's now working on ID'ing birds in flight.

I no longer worry that birdwatching is a static activity. It's turned out to be the most intellectually and physically rigorous thing I've ever done. It's also making me more self-sufficient. When I watch birds, I marvel at their endurance and their intrepid way of being in the world, and I want to replicate it. If that tufted duck managed to fly against the current, all the way to Hamilton, Ontario, figuring out a way to survive so far from his familiar surroundings and possibly learning a new dialect in the process, surely I can amass enough muscle to carry a scope. I gain strength from watching birds. It's not a passive pursuit. It is changing my life.

RECENTLY, WE HAD SOME OF LEON'S GYM FRIENDS OVER.

"So I heard you're working out," his friend said.

"It's a modest undertaking. I just really want a scope."

"No, it's still a workout."

Best of all, I could now follow their conversation about squats and deadlifts, since I was doing both, albeit with a fraction of their weights. We had a new shared vocabulary. Though Leon and I are still different species, my scope-training has unexpectedly given us something new to talk about. I'm not sure I'll ever graduate beyond the three-pound weights, but Leon offers constructive criticism and lifting tips whenever he sees me working out. And he no longer seems to mind that I yawn as I go.

Who knows which duck will appear in southern Ontario next year? I have to be prepared. And if I'm not ready, I'll keep trying.

Going Solo

SOMETHING HAPPENS WHEN YOU SEE THE SAME PEOPLE every Saturday over the course of many years. They become a sort of surrogate family, and then, as with all families, baggage starts to accumulate. For eight years, I was a member of a fantastic bird group. It remains an excellent group, led by one of the most dedicated and knowledgeable birders I've ever met. But somewhere along the line, I started to change.

A few years ago, I forced myself out the door three mornings a week to nearby Earl Bales Park during spring migration. To see if I could find a bird on my own. The joys were modest at first. A Baltimore oriole here, a yellow warbler there, nothing too remarkable. And then I recognized the descending scale of a downy woodpecker and caught sight of a red-tailed hawk flying overhead. Every time I went out alone, I compiled my list and lamented its brevity compared with the lists I had when I went out with my bird group. Would I be able to do this on my own if the only birds I could safely ID were also the ones that any non-birder could point out?

With every trip to the park, I started to see a little more. I finally grasped the difference between a downy and a hairy woodpecker, even though it had been explained to me at least a dozen times before. Although the hairy is larger, they look virtually identical in the field except for a crucial field mark that I had never internalized until I saw two of them in adjacent trees and figured it out for myself: the bill of the hairy is as long as his head is wide. That day, even though my species list barely broke double digits, I felt satisfied. Within a month of going to the park three times a week, I felt like I'd reached a certain level of familiarity with the birds, and I started to think of them as mine. I knew the specific branch that the belted kingfisher liked to perch on before he took off for his trans-marshy flight, rattling all the way to the other side. I knew to expect a hundred or so robins in the sumac trees and discovered which tree yielded the highest concentration and diversity of warblers. I found the black-and-white warbler's beloved tree trunk, the palm warbler's low bush and the northern parula's cherished treetops.

I repeated the experiment this past winter at Tommy Thompson Park, where the snowy owls were reliable from January to late April. I visited the park most weekends and saw the same three or four owls reclining in their trusted locales. One fancied the marina docks, another took to the rocks on the beach, and still another preferred the lighthouse. Just to keep me on my toes, they mixed it up a little, but every time I went out, I eventually saw them. By the end of winter, I started referring to them as "my owls."

The more I birded in Toronto, the more the city came alive for me. Even though I didn't know where the cool brunch spots were, I knew where the birds were, which turned out to be just as exciting for me. The city transformed from a traffic-congested concrete mass into pockets of green space, urban wilderness and abundantly fertile terrain for bird life.

I shuttled back and forth between my solo forays and trips farther afield with Brete's group. Slowly, the weekend trips that involved more driving than walking began to weigh on me. I wasn't enjoying them as much as I wanted to. What I really wanted to do, it turned out, was master the birds in my city. Birding was helping me develop affection for Toronto, the place I'd always wanted to flee, and that might have been the biggest surprise of all.

I had started out as a complete novice; I'd never noticed a bird beyond a pigeon, and now suddenly I had a birding philosophy. I found myself wanting to bird in a particular way. Birding with Brete showed me the possibilities, but now I wanted to narrow the scope. I was tired of always wanting to move somewhere else. The reality is that I won't be leaving Toronto anytime soon; the traffic won't be easing up anytime soon either. Discovering that I can watch American woodcocks perform their aerial spectacle in a park downtown, and that I can observe a wood thrush with its majestically polka-dotted breast as it intones its mellifluous song within ten kilometres of my home has made me look at the city through new eyes. The most unexpected fringe benefit of birding has been falling in love with my own city.

I quickly realized that I was never going to be a feverish lister; I just didn't care enough to compile a list that would, at best, get me a mention in the American Birding Association's newsletter. I keep a list, but I only include birds that I've gotten a good look at. If a guide mentions a bird, or hears one, I leave it off my list. I wasn't going to be an inspired twitcher either.

As I was transitioning into more of a local birder, my bird group strayed farther and farther from Toronto. I enjoyed the ten-kilometre walks and the avian surprises that came with them, while Brete's group preferred driving long distances to bird beyond the city, with limited time spent walking. Car birding has its advantages, and I'm not averse to it on occasion, depending on the species and the season, but I realized that what I loved most about birding, in addition to seeing the birds, was spending time outdoors, and coming home pleasantly exhausted.

But what I feared more than the differences in our birding styles was that I had started to rely on Brete's eyes and ears. I'd become a little lazy in my pursuit, knowing that I was in the company of someone with superior skills and attention. At a certain point, I reached a plateau, stopped asking questions and neglected to do the work of *really looking*.

"I don't think I can do it," I told Leon. "I won't be able to find the birds myself."

"Try. You probably know more than you think."

I still go out regularly on bird walks and often bird with Martha and Monika, but I don't think I'll join another bird group.

The first times I went out on my own, I felt at a loss. There was nobody for me to talk to, nobody to pat me on the head when I correctly ID'd a bird, or to correct me when I erred. Nobody to point out behavioural tendencies in birds or intricacies of plumage. For eight years, I'd had a personal birding coach—our group was small, rarely larger than five people—and now I had to do the looking for myself.

Over all these years of birding, I'd been accumulating field guides. I had my beloved Sibley, as well as Crossley, National Geographic, Peterson, Kaufmann, and early-twentieth-century field guides by Frank Chapman and Mabel Osgood Wright. I had tomes on sparrows, shorebirds, warblers and raptors, and my most recent acquisition, a field guide to birds of Ontario written in 1886. These field guides occupied a privileged spot on my bookshelf, but most of them remained untouched.

"What if nobody cares about my birding development?" I said to Leon.

"They probably won't."

"But that's so depressing." Essentially, he was telling me to grow up.

"What are you after? A gold star? You're forty-three years old. Can't you just bird for yourself?"

What did that even mean? I was married to a person with zero craving for external recognition. He lifted heavy things because it made him happy, and he wrote complicated code because it made a system work at its most efficient.

And me? I liked being the star pupil. Leaving Brete's group pained me. I'm not sure I'll ever find someone as invested in my birding progress as he was. I met him at the right time.

Becoming an unaffiliated birder meant that I was doing it for myself, since there wasn't any external recognition to be had. But when I could no longer rely on someone to give me all the answers, I started looking for them myself. I went through my field guides and determined that I preferred Sibley for the diversity of his depictions and the way he pinpointed distinguishing field marks. He managed to put himself in the shoes of a beginner. After Sibley, my heart belongs to the National Geographic guide for its pan-North-American versatility. Sometimes I confirm my sightings by cross-referencing eBird checklists posted by trusted birders in the area.

There's a thrill to finding the birds myself. I recently saw a trio of hairy woodpeckers drumming so vigorously, in syncopated rhythms, that I nearly called my drummer-brother-in-law to have him assess the musicality of the sequence. I don't always find the birds. I'm sure I miss more birds than I actually get.

I'M STILL NOT SURE WHAT KIND OF BIRDER I AM. WHEN A striking rarity along the lines of a fork-tailed flycatcher appears in Toronto, I'm a twitcher. When I volunteer at the bird banding station, I'm a (partial) extractor and a dedicated scribe. When I walk along the ravine near my house, I feel very much like a backyard birder, observing the behaviour of species in my vicinity. When I do a Christmas Bird Count, I feel like a birdy maniac. When I come home after hours in the field and proceed to write down all my sightings, along with their alpha codes and their Latin binomials, I sense the beginnings of listing hysteria gripping me. When I join an Ontario Field Ornithologists or Toronto Ornithological Club trip, I feel like a caricature of a birder, standing amidst a group of multipocketed-vest-clad people, all pointing our binoculars, as if on command. When I walk the length of the Leslie Street Spit, I feel very much like an urban birder, which is a subgenre in and of itself. In a way, I am all of these things.

You'd think that all my years of schooling would have taught me independence, but it took birding to really teach me what it means to go out into the field alone, and the strength and anxiety that comes with the territory.

I'm no longer searching for a Bird God with all the answers. I now want to find the answers myself.

The Tufted Wood Thrush

ONCE THE WINTER OF THE TUFTED DUCK CAME TO AN END, we took a spring trip to Washington, DC, where all I could talk about was the tufted titmouse. I make great efforts to see the bird in southern Ontario, but in DC it's a backyard bird, and I was rewarded with dozens of sightings. After the titmouse, I started fantasizing about a wood thrush, because we had just seen a hermit thrush, and I immediately wanted the next best thing, and also because I remembered that the song of a wood thrush sounds fluty and beautiful, though I couldn't sing it if I tried.

"Your birds are ruining my image," Leon said.

We had joked that all his talk about a harlequin duck sighting had emasculated him in the eyes of his friends.

"Which image?"

"My manly macho image."

"Right. The manly macho guy who bought a unicorn poster and maintains a collection of stuffed animals." One of the reasons I married Leon is that he is unclassifiable. "You could be the first powerlifting birder."

"No thanks," he said. "Birds are your thing."

And yet Leon often joins me, as long as it's an afternoon outing and he doesn't have to wake up early. He still says he won't ever carry my scope, but sometimes I catch him on Zeiss or Swarovski websites, becoming familiar with the finer points of optics and researching which model would be best. He won't yet let me book full-day birding excursions when we travel, but we both know that it's just a matter of time before we travel somewhere exotic that warrants more than a half-day in the field. And then there will be no turning back.

Leon has learned to cope with my birding anxiety crises and to understand the intense disappointment I feel when things don't go as planned. When I dwell on the bird I failed to see, he reminds me of everything I've already seen.

On a trip to Newfoundland in 2013, I had booked a bed and breakfast in Witless Bay for its porch overlooking the ocean. Within our first two days, I'd managed to see most of my target pelagic birds, except for puffins, without leaving the property, and I smugly texted Martha, "Saw a common murre," "Make that a dozen murres," "Razorbills sailing by," "Gannet performing nose-dive right now." And then, over breakfast on our third morning, I found out about Cape St. Mary's. I'd been so focused on seeing Atlantic puffins that I hadn't properly researched the fabled Bird Rock, home to one of the largest colonies of northern gannets in North America, and our itinerary was such that we couldn't accommodate the day-long detour.

"But you just saw a gannet."

"I know, but I could have seen over a thousand of them on one rock."

"We saw it plummet into the water right off our porch, I'm not sure what more you could want."

"I want a million gannets all together in one place."

Birding makes me insatiable. The more I see, the more I want to see. The first time I read about Phoebe Snetsinger, I thought she was dangerously obsessive. She started off going on a couple trips a year and eventually was travelling almost every month, to the point of missing her daughter's wedding for a rare bird in Indonesia. But sometimes I notice shades of that in myself.

And here we were, so close. If only I'd done more research before our trip to Newfoundland, if only I'd contacted more birders and put my time on Twitter to better use. If only.

On our penultimate day in Witless Bay, I woke Leon up at 6:00 a.m. with a plan: if we leave in half an hour, we could be at Cape St. Mary's by 10:30, spend a few hours communing with the northern gannets and be back before dusk when the moose would be a danger on the roads.

"You're crazy."

"Come on, why don't you want to do anything spontaneous?"

"Because this is nuts." And he rolled over and went back to sleep. I could have predicted this response. Leon hated long car rides; we would be flying across the island to Deer Lake in order to avoid the eight-hour drive, and here I was proposing at least an eight-hour car day for a bird we'd already seen.

I lay there seething, mentally divorcing him and running off with a more spontaneous option, someone who was willing to change his plans for the benefit of a hundred thousand gannets, someone who really understood me, someone who *really* loved birds and would be willing to rise with the sun and drive anywhere for them. Eventually

I exhausted myself with the divorce preparations and how I would explain all of this to my parents and grandmothers so they'd be unequivocally on my side, and fell asleep. When we woke up at a more reasonable hour, most of my ire had burned off, and over breakfast I heard people talking about a whale-watching and pelagic bird-watching guide named Captain Wayne, who went off the beaten path and took people out in zodiacs. I turned to Leon, fully expecting him to veto Wayne.

"Sure, call the captain."

And before I knew it, we had a pelagic trip booked for the afternoon. It turned out to be rainy, so we were the only ones who appeared on Captain Wayne's doorstep.

"It's raining. Are you sure you want to go out?" Wayne asked.

"Yes."

"Everybody else cancelled for this sailing. You'll get pretty wet."

"Wayne, we've been hiking in the rain for four days, so a few more hours in soaked pants isn't going to do any harm."

"Okay then, at your own risk. It'll be a bumpy ride." Poor Wayne; he was clearly going to lose money on this sailing.

We ended up getting a private tour of seabird paradise. Atlantic puffins swarmed us and bombarded us with their dizzying flights. Elegant razorbills stood on the rocky cliffs, guarding their nests. I had once been thrilled to see *one* razorbill in Niagara-on-the-Lake when it confused Lake Ontario with the Atlantic Ocean, but now they dotted the rocks, along with common murres and black guillemots. Up close, I could see the razorbill's white-striped thick bill and the white line that runs from the bill to the eye. Leon pointed out each of the four gannets we saw and I wondered whether he had called them beforehand to ensure their on-schedule arrival as a way of making me regret the whole Cape St. Mary's business. There were also minke and humpback whales, but we were too engrossed in watching the near-collision flight paths of the puffins to give the whales the attention they deserved.

At the end of our trip, I felt bad that Wayne had probably lost money on us and I bought one of his baseball caps.

"When are you going to wear that?" Leon asked afterwards, dismayed that I had bought a black hat monogrammed with "Captain Wayne."

"Maybe you'll want to wear it?" This was code for "I've just bought a really ugly hat and I have no idea why I did it but maybe you'll save the day and claim it as a gift." My gift giving was often suspect, and Leon knew it.

"Right. A black hat for summer. Great idea."

"I have good memories of Captain Wayne. I don't regret supporting his business."

"I don't either. But couldn't you have bought the light grey one?" Leon had a point, as usual. It's now been five years—I've never worn the hat, as predicted, but every time I open my closet and see Captain Wayne I think of the puffins and the seven northern gannets we saw—instead of the thousands we could have seen—and I think of how, if Leon had been someone else, he might have reminded me that had we gone in search of the gannets, we wouldn't have seen the puffins, but instead he never mentioned them again.

ON OUR LAST DAY IN DC, LEON WOKE UP AND ASKED ME IF tufted wood thrushes exist.

"I don't think so."

"Can you Google it?"

"It doesn't exist," I said. A quick search confirmed what I already knew.

"Did you look on a reputable website?"

"Yes. The Cornell Lab of Ornithology." He couldn't argue with that one.

"Well, I just had a nightmare about a tufted wood thrush. See what your birding has done to me? There were also two Kandinsky paintings." Leon now had non-existent bird species infiltrating his dreams, which my forensic psychiatrist friend jokingly diagnosed as subconscious PTSD. "Maybe someone has yet to discover it. The tuft was really cute—better than the one on that titmouse."

With his sci-fi/fantasy background, Leon is always on the lookout for rare or extinct species making a comeback.

Change happens imperceptibly. First the binoculars, then the odd birding trip while on vacation, then a conversation with a bird guide in Arizona, whom I'd asked to organize a low-intensity half-day tour because my husband wasn't a birder.

"So you're an SOB," the guide said, without missing a beat.

"A what?" Leon asked.

"Spouse of a Birder." There was no turning back. A new identity had been bestowed upon him.

But here we were, ten years later, with birds firmly enmeshed in the fabric of our lives.

THE THING ABOUT BIRDING IS THAT YOU NEVER KNOW exactly what you're going to see. Birding builds comfort with spontaneity. When I go out, I can have a checklist, but what I ultimately see depends on the bird's mood at that particular moment in time. Sometimes birds have other, more exciting plans. But sometimes, when I least expect it, a belted kingfisher sits still for me on the top branch of a tree, pausing between rattles and flights over the pond. And sometimes I wait for hours for a Eurasian tree sparrow, only to see nothing in the end. And even those days when nothing happens—when it's patience for the sake of patience, when I scan nearly a thousand house sparrows for the lone specimen that looks slightly different from all the rest—even those days are worth it to me, because when else would I gain such intimate knowledge of house sparrows?

Birding is teaching me to see things optimistically. To see and watch a bird is to be attuned to the moment itself. To follow a flight path with my binoculars is to be forever surprised because it never ends up where I might have planned.

I began birding tentatively, not sure what the point of it was. I couldn't see myself belonging to the multipocketed-vest club, and I had to take a year off after my initial grebe-fiesta in freezing weather when I managed to see exactly none of the birds in question. As my hairdresser, Randy, put it, "So you see a bird, and then what?" Did I really need a hobby that amounted to close observation for the sake of...nothing?

I kept coming back because watching birds made me happy. But I had no idea why. I had no idea that my life was about to change completely, because for the first time I would be looking into the details of things, examining a bird in its ecological context, falling in love with nature, and suddenly the world would expand and this place I lived in, which I had never found all that spectacular, this urban concrete mess laced with traffic, would come alive and transform into a series of interconnected wild spaces.

Even though I will always be a migratory species, somewhere deep down, seeing that bird, which might take off at any second, has taught me to sit still, to relish the moment. You see a bird, I'd now say to Randy, and then life becomes exponentially richer because suddenly you're connected with these magical flying machines that transport you back in time, since they're as close as you'll ever get, evolutionarily speaking, to dinosaurs. You see a bird as mesmerizing as the yellow-headed blackbird and you can't look back, you've fallen in love and want to do everything to protect them, and suddenly most of your cynicism washes away and you sense the fragility of their habitats, the challenges of their migrations and their ferocious determination to survive.

And when you really see that bird, the one that takes hold of you, the world appears full of wonder.

Coda: My Birding cv

I FINALLY JOINED THE TORONTO ORNITHOLOGICAL CLUB THE year they abandoned the "birding cv" as a criterion for eligibility. But for a few years before joining, I kept a draft of a birding resumé on my desk.

Spark bird: Red-winged blackbird, first seen at age thirty-five.

Nemesis bird: Bohemian waxwing. Seen once when her feet were freezing and she wasn't quite sure what it was and wondered why people cared so much about an overgrown, greyish cedar waxwing.

Birding education: Started out as a weekly birder on Saturdays, now carries binoculars everywhere.

Avian literature experience: Buys anything with "birds" in the title. Reads voraciously but isn't able to keep up with purchasing. Proud owner of field guides dating back to 1886 and books about most avian families.

Field experience: Survived a week on Stratton Island in Maine, monitoring breeding tern populations. Travelled to Maine in search of her wild side, which unfortunately she was unable to locate.

Volunteer experience: Tommy Thompson Park Bird Research Station's most talented scribe. Occasional releaser of birds. Even more occasional extractor of birds from mist nets.

Bird identification qualifications: Misidentifies most things with gusto.

Ability to identify by song: See above. Partial mastery of the songs of a yellow warbler, song sparrow, red-winged blackbird, American robin, northern cardinal, nuthatch sp. (though she's unable to distinguish between the red-breasted and white-breasted), Baltimore oriole. Can identify most things on a square block in Toronto in winter.

Wardrobe assessment: All T-shirts and sweatshirts are bird themed; sandpiper dress; barn owl skirt; wild hen scarf; hand-knit mittens with an unfamiliar Old World species, which an omniscient fellow birder convincingly identified as bullfinch.

Interior decorating style: Condo filled with bird art, including posters, paintings, Audubon clock, and bird-shaped stuffed animals, calendars, sculptures and handbags. Many items reflect a particular penchant for chickens.

Power animal: American woodcock for its fetching pout, eyes that can see backwards as well as forwards, and superhuman aerial acrobatics performed to attract a mate.

Favourite bird: Whatever bird she's looking at.

Ability to spread the birding gospel: Husband talks to his powerlifting buddies at the gym about the wonders of a harlequin duck while wearing a T-shirt with a giant American crow on it. Grandmother resorted to stealing a copy of the Golden Field Guide *Birds of North America* from her apartment building's common-room library. Sister and friends buy her bird-themed gifts. Everybody she knows e-mails with bird questions or sightings.

Birding/life aspirations: To sport the hairdo of a cedar waxwing, acquire the wardrobe of a northern flicker and develop the confidence of a Ross's goose.

Additional information: Likely a lifelong beginner birder.

Acknowledgements

I'M GRATEFUL TO THE RED-WINGED BLACKBIRD I SAW TEN years ago, which set this mad project in motion and changed my life in ways I couldn't have foreseen. And I'm grateful to every bird I've seen since, and all the ones I have yet to see. It's a good thing there are approximately ten thousand bird species in the world: I'll never be bored.

Immense gratitude to the following organizations and exceptional humans:

· To the Canada Council for the Arts and the Ontario Arts Council for financial support and for believing in my project.
· To the editors of *Orion Magazine* and *The Threepenny Review*, for publishing my essays, parts of which appear in a different version in this work. Thanks also to Susan Scott, editor of the anthology *Body & Soul: Stories for Skeptics and Seekers*, for publishing "Saved by a Red-winged Blackbird" and indulging my continued obsession with the red-winged blackbird.
· To Brush Creek Foundation for the Arts, for providing much-needed time and space to write, in stunning Wyoming, in addition to daily mountain bluebird sightings. Particular thanks to Sharon and Caitie for running a

fantastic artist residency, and for encouraging me to buy my first pair of (lime green) cowboy boots. Daily hikes and conversations with Rebecca Schultz made my weeks in Wyoming even more spectacular.

· To my Grade 5 teacher, Yvon Raoul, for teaching me the importance of rewriting. Thanks to you and Valerie for decades of friendship and laughter and for inviting us to your beautiful home on Denman Island, where I first read about "semi-retired hens" in the island newspaper; the hens found their way into my book and gave my writing group its name.

· To David Reed, my high school English teacher, for your faith in my early writing and for taking the words of a fifteen-year-old seriously.

· To Eugene Di Sante, for awakening my curiosity about all things ancient, archaeological, Italian and literary.

· To my ballet teachers, especially Marq Frerichs and Philip Payne, for giving me the confidence to stand straighter.

· To my Yiddish teacher extraordinaire, Ana Berman, for not falling asleep while I regale you with my weekly disquisition about birds *oyf Yiddish*. Apologies for my continued grammatical errors.

· To Maureen Stanton: meeting you at Colleague Circle was the best thing that happened to me (and my writing) in Missouri.

· To my dear hens here in Toronto—Samantha Garner, Teri Vlassopoulos, Lindsay Zier-Vogel—your generous feedback (and chips!) made this a better book.

· To my BBFs (Best Birding Friends), Monika Croydon and Martha Scott, thanks for being part of the story.

· To Rick Wright, for taking my words about birds seriously, and for suggesting that I write book reviews for *Birding*.

· To Brete Griffin and Heather Blakelock, for your patience, encouragement and knowledge.

· To Justin Peter, for turning me into a Christmas Bird Count addict.

· To the amazing birding organizations that have helped me along the way, including the Toronto Ornithological Club, Ontario Field Ornithologists and American Birding Association.

· To Nigel Shaw and the entire Tommy Thompson Park Bird Research Station crew, for continuing to welcome me season after season at the banding station. There is nobody I'd rather talk plumage with.

· To my fabulous agent, Kelvin Kong, for embracing this unintentional birder and helping her soar.

· To Anna Comfort O'Keeffe and the whole team at Douglas & McIntyre, for your passion, steadfast belief in my writing and my thoughts about avian hairdos, and your expertise. Special thanks to Becky Pruitt MacKenney, Merrie-Ellen Wilcox and Corina Eberle. It is a pleasure to work with you. Colossal thanks to my editor, Caroline Skelton, for your laser-sharp vision.

· To my beloved friends, for providing on-demand pep talks and for supporting my writing over the years: Amanda Irwin Wilkins, Elizabeth "Animal" Bowen, Chantelle Marshall, Rimma Garn, Tricia Khleif, Greg Foxman, Cole Crittenden, Brad Prager, Esther Marion, Bryn Canner, Laurel Glitherow, Kailan Rubinoff, Alina Iosif, Kathleen Whelan, Suzanne Alyssa Andrew, Maria Meindl, Kerry Clare, Rebecca Rosenblum and Carolyn Black.

· To Jessica Campbell and Elizabeth Campbell, dearest, oldest friends and steadfast correspondents, for making Vancouver continue to feel like home.

Acknowledgements

· To my cousin, Anna Fishzon, for being my first correspondent and for inspiring me with your courage, humour and brilliant words.

· To my sister, Ilana, for being my greatest cheerleader and providing me with two fabulous nephews whom I fully intend to indoctrinate and turn into bona fide bird nerds. Look out!

· To my grandmother, Nusya Markovskaya, for your fierce loyalty, your love of literature (and gossip magazines!) and your excitement about every single one of my publications. Even the birdy ones.

· To my in-laws, Markel and Svetlana, for your support and endless provision of cookies.

· To my parents, Inna and Boris, for setting an example, early on, of what it means to be a fearless artist, and also for providing me with endless material to write about. Thanks for calling me every time you see a "rare bird" in your backyard.

And final thanks to my husband, Leon Khankine, for wearing the SOB (Spouse of a Birder) badge with pride, and for supporting all my dreams, including the ones that require you to wake up at 4:00 a.m. This book is for you.

Birding Resources

SHOULD YOU FIND YOURSELF EAGER TO GET OUT INTO THE field and look for birds (and correctly identify them), here is a list of useful resources:

Recommended field guides

Dunn, Jon L., and Jonathan Alderfer. *National Geographic Field Guide to the Birds of North America*. Washington, DC: National Geographic Partners, 2017.

Sibley, David Allen. *The Sibley Guide to Birds*, 2nd ed. New York: Knopf, 2014.

Recommended reading

Ackerman, Jennifer. *The Genius of Birds*. New York: Penguin Books, 2016.

Birkhead, Tim. *Bird Sense: What It's Like to Be a Bird*. London: Bloomsbury, 2012.

Floyd, Ted. *How to Know the Birds: The Art and Adventure of Birding*. Washington, DC: National Geographic Partners, 2019.

Franzen, Jonathan. "My Bird Problem." *The New Yorker* (August 8, 2005).

Kaufman, Kenn. *Kingbird Highway: The Biggest Year in the Life of an Extreme Birder*. New York: Houghton Mifflin, 2006.

Maclear, Kyo. *Birds, Art, Life*. Toronto: Anchor Canada, 2017.

Weidensaul, Scott. *Living on the Wind: Across the Hemisphere with Migratory Birds*. New York: North Point Press, 1999.

Birding websites and apps

Cornell Lab of Ornithology: allaboutbirds.org
eBird: ebird.org
Larkwire: larkwire.com
Merlin Bird ID by Cornell Lab of Ornithology (app)
The Sibley eGuide to the Birds of North America (app)

Organizations doing important work to protect birds

Bird Studies Canada: birdscanada.org
American Birding Association: aba.org
Fatal Light Awareness Program (FLAP) Canada: flap.org
National Audubon Society: audubon.org

Citizen science projects

eBird: ebird.org
Christmas Bird Count: birdscanada.org/volunteer/cbc/
Christmas Bird Count 4 Kids: birdscanada.org/volunteer/
    cbc4kids/
Great Backyard Bird Count: gbbc.birdcount.org/